NORTH
KOREA

JAPAN

SOUTH
KOREA

C H I N A

TAIWAN

NEPAL

BHUTAN

BANGLADESH

I N D I A

BURMA

LAOS

CAMBODIA

VIETNAM

THAILAND

M A L A Y S I A

SRI LANKA

I N D I A

PAPUA
NEW GUINEA

I
N
D
O
N
E
S
I
A

A U S T R A L I A

CONTENTS

CONTENTS

THE HISTORY OF TEA

TEA AND ITS LEGENDS

It all began in 2737 BC in China. According to legend, whilst the emperor Shen Nung was boiling water to slake his thirst in the shade of a tree, a light breeze rustled the branches and caused a few leaves to fall. They mixed with the water and gave it a delicate colour and perfume. The emperor tasted it and found it to be delicious. The tree was a wild tea plant: tea was born.

In India, another legend tells of how Prince Dharma was touched by Divine grace and went out to preach the teachings of Buddha in China. To make himself worthy, he vowed never to sleep during the nine years of his journey. At the end of the third year, however, he was overcome by drowsiness and was about to fall asleep when by chance he plucked a few leaves from a wild tea plant and began to chew them. The stimulating qualities of tea immediately had their effect; Dharma felt much more alert and thereafter attributed the strength he found to stay awake during the six remaining years of his apostolic mission to these leaves.

In Japan the story goes a little differently: after three years Bodhi Dharma, exhausted, ended up falling asleep while he prayed. On awaking, infuriated by his weakness and devastated by his sin, he cut off his eyelids and threw them to the ground. Some years later, on passing the same spot, he saw that they had given birth to a bush that he had never seen before. He tried the leaves and discovered that they had the property of keeping a person awake. He told the people around him about his discovery and tea began to be cultivated in all those places through which he travelled.

Legends aside, it seems that the bush was originally from China, probably from the region around the border between north Vietnam and Yunnan province, and that the drinking of this beverage was first developed by the Chinese.

Since the invigorating and energising qualities of tea were very soon noted, it was at first used for medicinal purposes, either externally in the form of a paste to combat rheumatism or internally as a purifying soup. The first recipes for the preparation of tea were not too far from this idea: the leaves, which had been softened by steam, were ground with a mortar and pestle and compressed into flat cakes which were then brought to the boil with rice, milk, spices and sometimes even onions!

THE HISTORY OF TEA

TRADITION AND SYMBOLISM

During the Chinese Tang Dynasty (618–907 AD) the drinking of tea evolved into a more popular pastime, moving away from the realm of pharmacology and becoming a refined part of everyday life.

Teahouses came onto the scene and for the first time tea was a source of artistic inspiration: painters, potters and poets created a sophisticated universe around tea, laden with symbolism. One of them, Lu Yu (723-804 AD), drafted the first treatise on tea, *Cha Jing* or *Traditions of Tea*, a poetic work in which he describes the nature of the plant and standardises the methods of preparing and drinking the beverage. '*One finds*, he writes, *in the serving of tea the same harmony and order that govern all things*.'

Tea then was made of compressed briquettes, which were first roasted before being ground to a powder and mixed with boiling water. Some ingredients were then added: salt, spices, rancid butter... Tea is still taken this way in Tibet today.

During the Song Dynasty (960–1279 AD) a second school was born that, insofar as the lyricism of its ceremonies and the importance attached to the rules of preparation were concerned, was a precursor to the Japanese Cha No Yu School. The teas used were increasingly refined and fine china began to play a decisive role in the world of tea. The leaves were ground, with a mortar and pestle, to a very fine powder on to which the simmering water was poured. The mixture was then whipped until frothy with a bamboo whisk. Alongside this ritual, reserved for the court, a more widespread consumption of tea was developed, including other social classes. The first unpackaged, loose teas made their appearance and it was therefore possible to meet the growing popular demand.

THE HISTORY OF TEA

During the Ming Dynasty (1368–1644 AD) an imperial decree prohibited the manufacture of compressed tea and tea began to be taken in its present form: a brew in a pot. This new way of enjoying tea influenced the artefacts and accessories that were used in its preparation: it marked the beginning of earthenware and china tea sets. The kettle replaced the tea bottles of the Tang era and the teapot became the ideal receptacle to infuse the tea. Tea was being democratized and it gradually gained a following in every social class, enjoying even greater economic success with the start of the export trade.

In Japan tea appeared in the 7th century AD. On repeated occasions Buddhist monks brought tea plant seeds from China and tried to establish a tea growing culture in their country. However, it wasn't until the 15th century that tea was grown all over the archipelago. Sen No Rikyu (1522–1591 AD) was the first grand teas master: with him tea became a religion, an art and a philosophy. These disciplines were expressed through a complex and highly codified ceremony in which the ideal was to demonstrate the grandeur contained in the smallest everyday acts. 'Tea is no more than this,' he writes, boil the water, prepare the tea and drink it properly.'

EUROPE DISCOVERS TEA

From the 10th century onwards, tea was an export of primary importance for China: firstly to other Asian countries and then, starting in the 17th century, to Europe.

In 1606, the first tea chests arrived in Amsterdam in Holland: this was the first known cargo of tea to be registered at a western port. The East Indies Company, a Dutch firm, had close links at the time with the Far East and they maintained a monopoly over the sale of tea until the end of the 1660s, even after the creation, in 1615, of the East India Company, an English competitor. In 1657, Thomas Garraway, the landlord of a coffee house in London, introduced tea on his premises and placed an advert in the local paper which read: 'This excellent beverage, recommended by all Chinese doctors, and which the Chinese call 'Tcha', other nations 'Tay' or 'Tee', is on

THE HISTORY OF TEA

sale at Sultaness Mead *close to the Royal Exchange in London.'*

If the spread of tea at first met strong opposition — it was said to cause men to lose height and good humour, while women lost their beauty — it soon became the basis of a very important trade. At first the privilege of princes, it later became the favourite of all the dandies who frequented the 'coffee houses', soon to be re-named 'tea houses'.

Cromwell imposed a heavy tax on tea just before his death, and it quickly became the subject of a thriving contraband trade. In the 18th century its price became more accessible and tea became a revered national drink.

In France the introduction of tea gave rise to numerous controversies, from 1650 onwards, in medical circles. It therefore became extremely popular. In one of her letters Madame de Sévigné mentions that Madame de la Sablière was the first person to add tea to her milk. Racine was a faithful tea supporter, as was Cardinal Mazarin who drank it to treat his gout.

■ TEA CONQUERS THE WORLD

English and Dutch settlers brought tea to the New World, where it was to play a important role in the history of the United States. The commodity was subject to a very high duty and, in 1773, the inhabitants of Boston decided to boycott its import. On the 16th December they threw the cargo of a vessel anchored in the harbour into the sea: it was this 'Boston tea party' that provoked reprisals by the British authorities against the inhabitants of Massachusetts which, in turn, paved the way for the events that led to the War of Independence.

Tea was also the cause of more peaceful confrontations: like those of the tea clippers, light sailing ships used to transport tea.

In the 19th century the huge demand intensified rivalry between ship-owners: great races took place along the main maritime routes of the East.

The Chinese were the sole producers at the time and imposed their rules: prohibitive prices, limited access to the port of Canton and a refusal to exchange tea for English textiles. To counter this commercial pressure the English decided to illegally introduce opium into China to create dependence – and therefore give them some bargaining power – on the part of their business partner. This was the start of the Opium Wars that would end with Britain annexing Hong Kong in 1842.

By the 19th century China could no longer cope with the ever-increasing western demand and in 1830 the English started to develop tea cultivation in other countries. Tea plantations were started in India in 1834 and in Ceylon in 1857. The Ceylonese plantations at first were purely experimental but, in 1869, after the total destruction of coffee plantations by a parasite, tea became the island's main source of income.

Tea was also planted in other Asian countries that have become important producers; also in ex-British colonies in Africa and, more recently, in Reunion Island and in Argentina.

Today, tea is the most drunk beverage in the world after water, we drink about 15,000 cups every second.

The most important tea producing nations are (by percentage of world production):
• China (including Taiwan): 29%
• India: 26%
• Kenya: 9%
• Sri Lanka: 9%
• Turkey: 6%
• Indonesia: 5%
• Vietnam: 3.6%
• Japan: 2.5%

This is for a world production of 3,6 millions tonnes in 2006.

Reference: FAO, Intergouvernmental Group on Tea, 2006.

To find out more we recommend the publication by Paul Butel, 'Histoire du Thé' (in French), Desjonquières, Paris, 1989. Ref. L017.

THE TEA PLANTATION

Tea plantations look like a huge forest made up of small trees that rarely reach above 1.5m in height. When their trunks are thick and gnarled, they show that their age is much greater than their small size would suggest.

In their natural state tea plants can reach a height of 591 to 787 in. If they are to be cultivated they are kept at a height of about 47 in by regular pruning, in order to form what is known as the 'plucking table', which facilitates hand plucking and encourages bud growth.

Pruned and shaped by man over 50 or so years, the tea plants become real dwarf-trees and form strange plantations, a mixture of massive green covers and miniature forests.

THE TEA PLANT

The tea plant belongs to the Camellia family. There are two main varieties of the *camelia sinensis* or *thea sinensis*: the Chinese type, known as *sinensis*, with small and olive green leaves; and the Assam variety, known as *assamica*, which has large, pale, plump leaves. Other varieties have now appeared as a result of hybridization, grafting, propagation from cuttings etc, with many hybrids known as *jats* or *clonals*.

The cultivated tea plant is a bush with evergreen leaves, the upper surfaces of which are shiny and the undersides matt and paler. The young leaves and buds are covered with a light, silvery down, hence their name known as 'Pekoe' after the Chinese word 'Pak-ho' which means 'fine hair' or 'down'.

THE TEA PLANTATION

ECOLOGY

The tea plant grows in regions where the climate is hot and humid with rain falling regularly throughout the year. It grows between 42° latitude in the Northern Hemisphere and 31° latitude in the Southern Hemisphere.

The main countries where it is grown are:

- in Asia: Bangladesh, China, India, Indonesia, Japan, Malaysia, Nepal, Sri Lanka, Taiwan and Vietnam
- in Africa: Cameroon, Mauritius, Kenya, Rwanda and Zimbabwe
- in South America: Argentina and Brazil
- around the Caspian and Black Seas: Georgia, Iran and Turkey.

The top average temperature is between 64°F and 68°F and should have little daily variations.

The climate has an affect both in the volume and the quality of the harvest. A climate too humid will give a lower quality, while a dry season can often bring higher quality harvests. High altitude also improves quality with a smaller yield. In tropical regions, the tea plant can be cultivated at altitudes ranging from sea level up to 1,55 mi.

Sunlight is important: it is necessary for the formation of the essential oils that give the brew its aroma. The light should preferably be scattered: this is why large trees are regularly planted on tea plantations, they regulate the soil ecology and filter the strong sunrays.

The soil should be permeable, loose and deep since the tea plant's roots can push down to a depth of up to 236 in. Soil cover should be at least 59 in deep. The best areas have a young, volcanic soil which is very permeable and rich in humus, neither basal nor too clayey. Tea is always grown on sloping ground, allowing for natural drainage, since the tea plants, unlike rice plants, cannot survive in stagnant water. This drawback is also a trump card: the tea plant is very resilient, it can be grown on extreme gradients and is perfectly suited to the most steeply-sloping, mountainous terrain.

THE TEA PLANTATION

CULTIVATION

Growing tea used to be done from seeds that were re-planted. Nowadays reproduction of tea plants is basically accomplished by taking cuttings from selected plants.

The cuttings are taken from the chosen plants and then replanted onto nursery beds where they will remain for 12 to 18 months. As soon as they turn into young plants, they are replanted in the main plantation, being spaced out in such a way that the fully grown bushes will cover the entire area when they reach maturity. The plant is left for 4 years before any leaves can be plucked. Constant pruning and shaping will form its required height of 47 in, hence creating *the plucking table* and giving

a good framework to the bush. It will not reach full growth until the fifth year when it will begin to produce. It will still be pruned at varying intervals — on average every two years — in order to keep it at a good height for plucking.

A mature tea plant does not usually live for more than 40 or 50 years. Nonetheless some varieties can live up to 100 years.

At the end of the fifth year, the tea plant is ready to be harvested. This operation, which consists of a light, repeated, pruning of the young shoots, is carried out in a 7 to 15 days cycle, depending on the growth, the climate and the amount of tea to be plucked.

Since the tea plant has evergreen leaves, plucking can be done all year round, except in the high altitude plantations where it only takes place from February to November.

Plucking seasons in Asia:

- China: February to November
- Northern India: February to November
- Southern India: all year round
- Indonesia: all year round
- Japan: 4 times a year, from May to October
- Sri Lanka: all year round except in high altitude
- Taiwan: mainly in Spring, summer and autumn.

TEA PLUCKING

A small bud forms at the end of each stem and quickly becomes a young shoot. This end leaf is usually curled and forms the bud.

Other leaves are found on the stem and their number below the bud will determine the quality of the plucking: the more are removed, the lesser quality plucking.

There are three types of plucking:

• the imperial plucking: the bud + the leaf that directly follows.
• the fine plucking: the bud + the two leaves that follow. This is a harvest of excellent quality.
• the average plucking: the bud + the three leaves that follow. This gives a lesser quality tea than the previous two but it allows the tea plant to grow better.

The leaves are never plucked separately: the part of the stem that unites the young shoot and the leaves is always plucked as a whole.

In order to obtain some much sought-after teas, the 4th and 5th leaves, also called Souchong, are picked. These are usually to be found in smoked Chinese teas.

After a certain period of time the tea plant will have stems with no young shoots. This marks the resting period. The end bud is formed of the 'deaf' leaf which is then removed in order to allow the stems to recover.

Plucking is still done, in the majority of cases, by hand. Mechanization of tea plucking is still very rare; with some exceptions however:

• in Japan scissors are used.
• also in Japan, and in Georgia, mechanized clippers are used to straddle the rows and pluck an area with a width of 59 in. This method presupposes a flat terrain and a large harvest, except in Japan where mechanization is very advanced but also very expensive.
• in Argentina, tractors are used.

To learn more about the agronomic aspects of tea cultivation, we recommend 'Le Théier' (in French) by Denis Bonheur, Maisonneuve et Larose, Paris 1989. Ref. L018.

The colours of tea

Green tea, black tea, white tea, dark tea or red tea: tea comes in all colours and each colour corresponds to a very particular type of tea. At the root of this diversity is just the one plant: the tea plant, but its leaves have been processed in different ways and have undergone numerous transformations. The most important of these is fermentation, a chemical reaction that takes place as a result of enzymes contained in the fresh leaf. By setting off and controlling this process the tea planter gives its selected colour to the tea.

Here are the secrets of the manufacture of different types of tea.

Green teas

Green teas are unfermented teas. Their preparation therefore aims to avoid any hint of fermentation. The leaves go through three processes: roasting, rolling and firing.

roasting

The purpose of roasting is to kill those enzymes in the leaves that cause fermentation. In order to do this, the leaves are brutally heated to a temperature of around 212°F, either in large pans (the Chinese method) or by steam cooking (the Japanese way), for anything from 30 seconds to 5 minutes. The leaves thus become soft and easily bendable for the rolling process.

rolling

The leaves are then rolled or folded by hand to give them the appearance of small sticks, balls, coils or actual tea leaves as is the case, for example with Long Jing tea. The operation can be carried out either hot or cold, according to the fineness of the harvest: young shoots are easily rolled cold since they have a high water content, as opposed to more mature leaves which require immediate rolling after the roasting process, while they are still hot.

Green tea from Japan
Gyokuro Hikari — Ref. 300

Black tea from China
Qimen Impérial — Ref. 223

Semi fermented tea from Taiwan
Dong Ding — Ref. 264

Smoked tea from China
Grand Lapsang Souchong — Ref. 240

White tea from China
Bai Mu Dan — Ref. 194

Dark tea from China
Pu Er Impérial — Ref. 215

THE COLOURS OF TEA

firing

The leaves are dried on racks called 'tats' with hot air being circulated for two or three minutes. Then this process stops for half an hour leaving the leaves to rest, after which time the drying is repeated until the moisture content of the leaves is no more than 5 to 6%.

WU LONG OR SEMI FERMENTED TEA

These are teas in which the fermentation has been interrupted mid-process. More mature leaves that therefore, contain less tannin and caffeine, are often used for this category of tea.

Wu Long (oolong) teas are a speciality of the Fujian province in China and of Taiwan. These Wu Long teas are currently divided into two categories: lightly fermented teas (10%-15% fermentation) prepared in the so-called Chinese way; and others where the fermentation process is much more important (60%-70%) in which the teas are processed according to a method more specifically developed in Taiwan. In practice, the preparation of semi fermented teas is an area less clear-cut than this: each plantation has its own recipes and produces teas with different degrees of fermentation, which does not necessarily correspond to these two categories. In order to classify Wu Long (oolong) teas then, this guide has opted to use a criteria that expresses the degree of fermentation rather than using the traditional divisions made according to Chinese versus Taiwanese methods. Whatever the end product and notwithstanding local wisdom, all semi fermented teas have to go through the following procedures:

withering

The leaves are left to wither in the sun for a few hours, and are then put in the shade to cool. The fermentation process begins.

sweating

This is the most important stage in the preparation of semi

fermented teas. The leaves are placed in a room that is kept at a constant temperature of between 72°F and 77°F, with a humidity level of roughly 85%, in which they are continually stirred with ever-increasing force. This allows the aroma to be released and facilitates the evaporation of water. The final degree of sweating depends on the duration of this process: in the so-called Chinese method the fermentation is halted as soon as the leaves have reached a 10%-12% degree of fermentation and this produces light teas with a leafy flavour. The so-called Taiwanese method involves a longer period of sweating allowing fermentation to progress to a level of up to 70% and producing darker, fruitier teas.

roasting

Once the desired degree of fermentation has been reached, roasting allows the tea enzymes' reaction to be halted. This procedure is identical to the one used to produce green teas.

rolling

As is the case for green teas, the rolling process will give the tea leaves their twisted shape. Naturally, the leaves are often very large and are just creased or sometimes rolled into large pearls, as is the case with Dong Ding teas.

WHITE TEAS

These are teas that have remained in their natural state. The leaves in this case only undergo two procedures: withering and firing. In order to obtain a level of moisture loss comparable to other teas, the leaves are left to wither for a much longer period of time: from 52 to 60 hours. They are then immediately dried in large pans for approximately half an hour. The process might appear simple but the production of white teas is nevertheless one of the most delicate. Withering in the open air is an operation impossible to control in terms of humidity and heat: the skill of the tea planter lies in accurately predicting weather conditions and organising the timing of the plucking accordingly. White teas are a Chinese speciality from the Fujian region.

THE COLOURS OF TEA

Black teas

For black teas the fermentation process is allowed to run its full course. Legend has it that in the 17th century, a cargo of green tea from China arrived in London after a particularly long voyage. During the journey the tea chests had gone mouldy and the tea they contained had turned from green to black. Not great tea connoisseurs, the English enjoyed it so much that they asked for a new delivery to the Chinese…

withering

This first procedure is to give to the leaf pliability for subsequent rolling. Fresh leaves lose 50% of their moisture. The harvest is spread out evenly on bamboo or hessian racks placed 5 to 7 in apart in a room. The room temperature is kept constant between 68°F-75°F with fans circulating air. This process usually takes between 18 and 32 hours.

rolling

The rolling of black tea differs from green teas: its objective is not to twist the leaf but to break down its cell structure, in order to facilitate the enzymes reaction of the fermentation. If the leaves are lightly rolled they will produce a mild tea; if they are more twisted the tea will have a more pronounced flavour. Rolling can be carried out either by hand or by machine.

fermentation

The leaves are sent next to the fermentation room. In these rooms the humidity ranges from 90% to 95% with a temperature from 68°F to 72°F. Ventilation needs to be good however without any draughts. The leaves are spread out in layers of between 2-2,3 in. Fermentation can last for anything from 1 to 3 hours, depending on the quality of the leaves, the season, the region and according to the strong colour desired.

THE COLOURS OF TEA

roasting

To stop fermentation the tea has to be brought to a high temperature as fast as possible.

Roasting usually takes place in large, cylindrical drying machines that heat the leaves to an average temperature of 194°F, for 15 to 20 minutes.

grading

The next thing that must be done is to sort the tea by grade. The tea is immediately sorted into two grades:
• broken leaves
• whole leaves
Broken leaves are obtained either naturally when, whole leaves are broken during handling, or artificially by being cut with a machine. Whole leaves are classified according to the fineness of the harvest.

SMOKED TEAS

Smoked teas are black teas. A Chinese story dates their appearance to around 1820 in the Fujian region. At this time the Chinese army had requisitioned a plantation. The plantation owner, having been told to free up the drying room, found himself with a considerable quantity of wet leaves. As he didn't want to lose them, he decided to dry them out quickly. He therefore lit a fire with some roots of a spruce tree and placed the leaves on it. The leaves dried in a few minutes and had a very particular smoked taste. A few days later a foreign trader, who happened to be visiting the planter, discovered this discarded batch of tea. He was seduced by its aroma and took it with him to Europe where it met with great success.

Nowadays, to produce smoked teas the same process is followed: after rolling, the leaves are lightly grilled on a hot iron sheet, then arranged on bamboo racks, above a spruce root fire. The length of this process depends on the level of smoking one wishes to attain. Smoked teas remain a speciality of the Fujian region and, like many teas from this area, they are also prepared in Taiwan.

THE COLOURS OF TEA

DARK TEAS

This type of tea, known as Pu Er, is produced with a steaming process that provokes a non-enzymatic fermentation, different from the black teas. Before being rolled, the leaves undergo a specific roasting, which kills most of their enzymes. This is done in iron pans, heated to 536°F-608°F, into which the leaves are placed and then covered with straw. The straw stops the steam from escaping and allows the leaves to be steam cooked. This is essential as the leaves are old and are lacking in moisture. During this operation, the caffeine of the leaves decreases. A first rolling is carried out, then the leaves are arranged in piles of about 1m high and covered with a damp cover to keep a hygrometric level of 85%. This is the sweating process. It lasts about 24 hours and can be repeated several times. The size of the piles and the duration of the sweating period have important consequences for the tea produced; its aroma will be more, or less, enhanced. Dark teas can often be found in the form of compressed bricks or bird's nests. They are also the only teas that improve with age and for which age can sometimes carry enormous weight when selling at auction.

'Discovering the cultures of the world' Gift box
12 tea samples from around the world. – Ref. DCME

THE COLOURS OF TEA

THE COLOURS OF CHINESE TEA

While in most countries the division of teas is confined to a distinction between green, black and semi fermented teas, Chinese teas have their own classification system that partially diverges from international criteria and is based on the colour of the infusion produced by the tea. The classification is built around the six great families of tea: green teas, blue-green teas, red teas, black teas, yellow teas and white teas. It reflects the diversity of Chinese teas and Chinese mastery in their fermentation. Indeed, each colour is the result of a very specific manufacturing process, allowing the tea leaf to undergo various degrees of fermentation, which, in turn, give to the tea its characteristic qualities of taste.

While the white and green teas correspond to those described previously, this is not the case for the others. The blue green teas are the same as semi fermented teas Wu Long (oolong) teas. Red teas are more commonly known as black teas. As for Chinese black teas, not to be confused with the aforementioned, they correspond to those teas that are classified as dark teas in the West. Finally, yellow teas are very rare and are close to green teas in terms of their method of production.

White tea – Aiguilles d'Argent - Ref. 193

Green tea – Ban Qiao Mao Feng – New season tea

Blue-green tea – Tie Guan Yin Impérial - Ref. 2165

Red tea – Yunnan d'Or - Ref. 219

Black tea – Pu Er Impérial - Ref. 215

The leaves of green and semi fermented teas are usually whole and the grade is not specified. The same applies for a few of the black teas, particularly Chinese, where its name is a synonym of quality. For other black teas the grade is important since it gives two pieces of information:

- the fineness of the crop,
- the size of the leaf (whole, broken, ground).

Whole leaves:
Saint-James O.P. - Ref. 111

In these grading the term 'orange' is not connected with the fruit of the same name. It means 'royal', and comes from the name of the Dutch dynasty *Orange Nassau*. As for the word Pekoe it comes, as you will remember, from the Chinese word *Pak-ho* meaning 'fine hair' or 'down', and denotes the end bud, which gives an impression of white down, since it is not entirely open.

whole leaves

F.O.P. Flowery Orange Pekoe

This is the finest crop of all. It is composed of the final bud and the following two leaves. The tea contains many buds that, after they have been browned during fermentation, are sometimes known as 'golden tips'.

Broken leaves:
Saint-James B.O.P. - Ref. 121

O.P. Orange Pekoe

These are young, tightly rolled

Ground leaves:
Saint-James Fannings - Ref. 180

eaves. The crop is fine but a little later than the previous one: in this case, the bud has already become a leaf.

P. Pekoe

The leaf is less fine than the O.P. and does not contain any buds.

S. Souchong

The leaves here are lower, larger, older and with a lower caffeine content; they are often rolled lengthwise and are used above all for smoked teas.

■ broken leaves

The leaf is no longer whole and is much smaller than the O.P. An infusion of this tea gives a much darker, stronger beverage.

B.O.P. Broken Orange Pekoe
F.B.O.P. Flowery B.O.P.
G.B.O.P. Golden B.O.P.
T.G.B.O.P. Tippy Golden B.O.P.

■ ground leaves

F. Fannings

Flat pieces smaller than broken leaves. The infusion produced is very strong and highly coloured.

Dust

Leaves not yet ground, mainly used for tea bags.

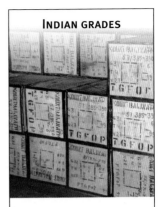

INDIAN GRADES

In northern India, the description of the crop is much more emphasized and gives a much more accurate indication of quality than in other countries.

- **G.F.O.P.** *Golden Flowery Orange Pekoe.*
F.O.P. has a high proportion of buds.
- **T.G.F.O.P.** *Tippy Golden Flowery Orange Pekoe.*
F.O.P. containing many golden buds.
- **F.T.G.F.O.P.** *Finest Tippy Golden Flowery Orange Pekoe.*
F.O.P. of exceptional quality.
- **S.F.T.G.F.O.P.** *Special Finest Tippy Golden Flowery Orange Pekoe. F.O.P. of the finest exceptional quality. A grade that is usually reserved for the best springtime Darjeelings.*

A number is sometimes added after the grade to classify, not the fineness of the crop, but the tasting quality of the tea obtained.

Tea and health

Ever since its first appearance in Asia, tea has been considered beneficial for the body. Its oldest references come from historians advocating its medicinal properties: at first tea was used in the form of a paste, as a poultice to combat rheumatism. Legends about tea, whether Chinese, Indian or Japanese, all show, in their own way, the stimulating and invigorating properties of tea. The Emperor Shen Nung, father of Chinese medicine and farming, states in his Medical Book that, *'tea relieves tiredness, strengthens the will, delights the soul and enlivens the sight.'*

In the 20th century medical science allows us to understand scientifically the many benefits that tea drinkers have known empirically for over two thousand years.

ALKALOIDS

There are three alkaloids present in tea: caffeine, theophylline and theobromine.

These are organic substances that are found in all types of teas whatever its colour.

caffeine

This is the main alkaloid in tea; it represents 2% to 3% of the dry leaf. It is important to realize that caffeine found in tea and coffee is one of the same molecule, the only difference being that it is proportionately more present in coffee.

The caffeine content of a tea depends both on the leaf used – the bud and the first leaf contain twice as much as Souchong leaves – and on the season of the harvest, since climatic variations influence the maturity of the leaf.
Some teas are therefore high in caffeine: new season crops, those with many buds; others are almost entirely bereft of caffeine: smoked teas and Wu Long (oolong) teas.

Caffeine is a strong stimulant to the nervous system. Unlike coffee, the caffeine in tea is released slowly into the body. Because of this, it allows us to stay awake and alert without becoming hyper. This makes tea the ideal beverage to accompany exercise, both mental and physical.

While this stimulating effect can cause a slight tendency towards insomnia in sensitive people it is very easy, on the other hand, to 'decaffeinate' one's tea at home without altering the flavour: because the caffeine in tea is a constituent which is released in the first few seconds of infusion, just rinse the leaves with a first pouring of boiling water, leave for about thirty seconds and then throw the water away.

theophylline

Theophylline is present in much smaller amounts than caffeine. Its function is essentially one of vasodilatation, in other words it helps to dilate veins and blood vessels, improving blood circulation. This explains why tea, whether ice cold or boiling hot, is a refreshing drink: vasodilatation is one of the mechanisms that contribute towards the thermoregulation of the body's temperature. Theophylline is also a respiratory stimulant, which is used in certain medicines for the treatment of asthma. However tea should not, under any circumstances, be considered as a remedy for this type of complaint.

theobromine

This alkaloid, which is found in lesser quantities than the previous two, has a strong diuretic effect. By stimulating renal circulation, it

encourages evacuation though the urinary tract.

TANNINS OR POLYPHENOLS

Tannins in tea are similar substances to the tannins found in wine, both have very similar properties. Some characteristics of tea, like its colour, its body or its strength, are directly dependent on these polyphenolic derivatives and on the changes they have undergone. It is easy to recognise a tea that is high in tannin by the astringency of the drink, which sometimes translates into bitterness if the tea has been over brewed: tannins are released slowly but in an ever increasing way, so that an overly long infusion considerably raises their concentration and makes the tea bitter.

Astringency plays a role in the tightening of cell tissue. Used externally, tea can be used in a

Tea and health

Tea and iron

It is often said that drinking tea lowers iron levels in the blood.

Indeed, the tannins present in tea, while being very beneficial to the body on many counts, do have one defect: they prevent the iron contained in foods from being totally absorbed by the body during digestion. A heavy daily consumption of tea (more than 1.5 litres) could have an effect on the body's absorption of iron. This does not pose a problem if the tea drinker does not suffer from an iron deficiency and has a well-balanced diet. If this is not the case, it is recommended to wait for 40 minutes after meals before drinking tea.

Iron absorbed by the human body is found in red meats and, to a much lesser extent, in vegetables. A vegetarian therefore has a greater risk of iron deficiency. Pregnant women are also more at risk: during this period it might be better to limit consumption of tea.

bath to close and tighten pores, or in the final rinse when shampooing hair to make it smooth and shiny.

The main polyphenolic derivatives of tea are catechols and flavonoids. Their effect on the human body has been particularly highlighted by research into green teas. The reason for this is that most scientific studies in this area have been carried out in Japan, a country that produces only green tea. However, in recent years this study has been extended to include other families of teas: black teas, Wu Long (oolong) teas and dark teas. While tannins are present in different types of tea, the fermentation process, on the other hand, changes them and the effects of polyphenols in non-green teas are still not well understood by researchers. Are they the same or are they different from those in green teas? We will have to wait a few more years before we have the answer.

Scientific research has revealed that polyphenols have an effect on bad cholesterol. Thus a daily intake of 5 cups of tea leads to a lowering, after a few months, of LDL-cholesterol - the 'bad' cholesterol as opposed to HDL-cholesterol.

Other studies have further explored this matter and have highlighted the effects of green tea in the prevention of cardio-vascular disease, especially arteriosclerosis, an arterial disease associated with hardening of the arteries and fatty deposits.

One digestive effect of polyhenols has been demonstrated: drinking green tea limits the absorption of fats during digestion. So a cup of tea taken at the end of a meal, about 40 minutes afterwards, will aid digestion by activating a process of fat elimination.

Numerous scientific theories pertaining to the antioxidizing effects of polyphenols have also been tested. Polyphenols, which are present in considerable quantities in fruit, vegetables, red wine and green tea, play a vital role in the fight against the free radicals that are responsible for the aging of cells. One of the polyphenols in green tea – epigallocatechol gallate – is the object of very detailed scientific research into the fight against the development of cancerous cells. This polyphenol might inhibit the actions of the enzyme, urokinase, which is responsible for the random multiplication of cancerous cells.

At the present time, this research has been tested only on animals, and the same results still have to be proven for man in order to establish a link between tea consumption and the prevention of certain cancers. It must be added, that this research is not, in any way, taking place within a therapeutic framework but solely in terms of preventative dietary guidelines.

VITAMINS

vitamin C

Tea is a plant with a naturally high vitamin C content (about 3,8gr per 3,5 oz of fresh leaves). Unfortunately, this is completely destroyed from the minute the

tea is infused in water at a temperature above 86°F. Tea cannot, therefore, be used as a source of vitamin C. On the other hand, flavonoids, one of the tannins found in tea, help promote the body's absorption of vitamin C.

vitamin P

Tea contains a considerable amount of vitamin P, which increases capillary strength and shortens bleeding time.

B group vitamins

Highly soluble in water, many B vitamins are to be found in a cup of tea. They contribute to the general good health of the human body, by kick-starting the metabolism, in other words the whole series of reactions taking place within our organic tissue: energy output, nutrition, assimilation…

MINERALS

Tea is rich in potassium and fluoride. On the other hand it is low in salt, which makes it perfectly suitable for salt-free diets.

The importance of fluoride in the fight against dental cavities is well known. Tea contains 0,3mg per cup. Since we know that we need to absorb 1mg of fluoride per day to protect our tooth enamel, tea can be an effective contributor, if taken regularly.

PREVENTION

In conclusion, we must emphasize, once again, the fact that all the properties and benefits of tea underlined here are dietary and not therapeutic recommendations. Drinking tea, in whatever quantities, should never be seen as part of the treatment for curing such or such a disease. But, regular tea drinking effectively contributes towards maintaining good health and to the prevention of some infections.

ORGANICALLY GROWN TEAS

Le Palais des Thés has a selection of organically grown teas of excellent quality, which have been specially certified.

In tea producing countries the idea of organic farming is still not very widespread. Nonetheless, for some years, the desire amongst some planters to promote their 'clean' agricultural methods has lead, to requests for the certification of their crops by bodies that generally operate in Europe.

Under the control of these bodies, the plantations in question are divided into two categories:
• those that already practise an environmentally friendly form of agriculture, in accordance with norms established by European entities: they can then enjoy the benefits from being certified, *organically grown*;
• those that, from a desire to restructure and improve their production methods, have under-taken to put a series of measures into place, as stipulated by the certifying body: certification will only be given once these measures have been complied with.

It should be specified that plantations earning an organically grown certification are rare and are the result of a conscious decision on the part of certain planters who are well informed and are prepared to finance regular controls of their crops by the certifying body. Nevertheless, those plantations that do not wish or are unable to make this type of financial undertaking, either because of their small size or other financial commitments or even because of their lack of understanding of this kind of farming, should not automatically be judged as less ecological than the others. It should be particularly noted that, in the case of private smallholdings, the planters often practise methods of farming which are totally free from any chemical products, since these are too expensive.

Le Palais des Thés encourages and supports this conscientiousness from the planters, imports a selection of certified teas under the french label, '*Agriculture Biologique*'. Since the teas can change from year to year — plantations are re-evaluated regularly — this selection features in the attached price list.

TEA TASTING

THE MECHANICS OF TASTE

During the tasting process our perception of the different sensations happens in three stages.

• The first contact with the tea is olfactory, through the nose: one begins by smelling the tea, deliberately or not, as soon as the cup is lifted towards the mouth. This type of olfaction, known as direct olfaction, provides only limited information about what we are about to drink. Indeed, when we inhale, only 10% of the molecules that have a smell reach our olfactory nervous cells. This percentage can be raised by a shorter, sharper intake of breath, which tea-tasting specialists refer to as 'sniffing'.

• The following stage takes place in the mouth, by taking a sip. Two senses are involved: taste and touch. As far as taste is concerned there are three possible flavours with tea: bitter, sour and sweet, each one being more or less discernible in different parts of the mouth. Our sense of touch is activated by contact with the mucous membrane and the teeth; it allows us to enjoy the texture and the temperature of the liqueur. It is at this moment that we can feel the astringency, the body and the smoothness of the tea. There has still been no perception of aroma though and from the point of view of taste, the information provided by this second step is still very limited.

• At the moment of swallowing retro-olfaction takes place, in other words an exhalation of air through the nose provokes a simultaneous inhalation of air through the mouth. This 'draught of air' completely cleans out the sensitive area of our olfactory apparatus and we can then smell 100% of the aroma molecules. To understand the importance of this step, one only has to hold one's nose at the moment of swallowing: in this way retro-olfaction does not happen and perception will be limited to the three flavour sensations described above.

It is indeed through smell that we perceive the essence of what we 'taste' and through smell that the aromatic complexity of a drink like tea is revealed.

TEA TASTING

PROFESSIONAL TASTING

In order to be able to bring you the best teas at the best times, our experts at Le Palais des Thés constantly tastes and compares dozens and dozens of different teas. Sometimes these tastings take place on the plantations themselves, whether they are in India, China, Japan etc., but also in Paris where, every week, Le Palais des Thés receives many hundreds of samples from each and every continent.

Just as wine, professional tea tasting follows a very precise ritual, the object of which is to highlight the best qualities and the defects of the tea, and often to compare the different batches produced from the same harvest. In whatever country the tasting takes place, it always follows the same rules and is carried out using the same instruments.

The taster begins by lining up in front of him all the samples he wishes to taste and compare. He spreads them out on large sheets of white paper, so that he can look at and smell each dry leaf and keep the file for each sample in the correct order. In this way he can always refer back to the information contained on each file: supplier's name, plucking date, plantation of origin, price, etc.

A WORD FROM AN EXPERT: FRANCOIS-XAVIER DELMAS
Founder of Le Palais des Thés

'For almost fifteen years now I have been lucky enough to travel along the tea routes, discovering plantations, meeting the men and women working there and seeking out the highest quality teas. So why actually go there? It is by walking up and down a plantation, by following every step in the treatment of the leaves that one learns the most about tea; it is by being there that we have access to the rarest and freshest teas; in short, by being there, we have been able to build up a network of solid and professional relationships in every tea-producing country.

A journey through a plantation is also an opportunity to observe the working conditions and the farming methods: are there weeds amongst the tea plants, is no deforestation taking place, is the ecosystem being respected, how does the plantation's healthcare centre work, are the children receiving proper schooling? These are some of the indications that allow us to evaluate and reassure ourselves of the quality of farming being practised and the living and working conditions on the plantation we are visiting.

Visiting the location is, in the final analysis, an opportunity for us to meet all the men and women who take part in the manufacture and the selling of tea... Tea is also the national drink in very many countries... I cannot imagine being interested in tea from solely a taste point of view and missing out on this wealth of human and cultural tradition... I would like to share this wealth with you; I would like to take you on a journey. And I hope your visit to Le Palais des Thés will be the first step.'

Tea tasting

For the preparation of tea, the expert uses a tasting kit. This is made up of three components: a bowl, a cup with a spout and its lid. During a tea tasting session as many kits are used as there are teas to be tasted.

In each cup, which he will then cover with its lid, the taster places 0,1 oz of tea onto which he pours about 0,1l of simmering water. The length of infusion can vary from anything from 1 minute for the most delicate green teas to 10 minutes for some white teas. Whatever the type of tea, the infusion lasts longer than it would in a teapot: this enhances the tea's characteristics and brings out its good and bad qualities. Respecting this condition sometimes comes at the cost of producing strong bitterness, but it is necessary, especially in the case of teas with very similar characteristics.

After some minutes of brewing, the taster pours the liquid into the bowl while holding the lid on the cup. In this way the leaves are held back and do not cloud the liqueur.

At the end of these preparations, the tea is available in three different states: as a dry leaf, in the infused state (in other words the soaked leaf) and as a liqueur. The tasting can now begin. For the wet and the dry leaf the expert evaluates:
• their appearance: size, colour, fineness of the crop, working of the leaf...
• their texture: softness and strength, the level of hygrometry in the case of the dry leaf,
• their scent: dry and infused notes,
For the liqueur, he will pay particular attention to:
• the colour and the clearness of the liquid,
• its feel in the mouth,
• its taste: the flavours and the aromas.

The taster's glossary that follows lists the vocabulary used by tasters and allows the sensations felt during the drinking of tea to be described.

A TASTER'S GLOSSARY

Technical Vocabulary

• **Aroma:** in the technical language of tasting, aroma should be reserved for the olfactory sensations felt in the mouth during retro-olfaction. But the word is also frequently used to describe smells in general.

• **Bouquet:** all the characteristics of smell that are perceived through the nose when one sniffs the tea, then in the mouth known as aromas.

• **Flavour:** sensation (sweet, salty, sour, bitter, glutinous) perceived on the tongue.

• **Infusion:** this refers both to the act of infusion and to the soaked leaves which one then retrieves. For tea it is never used to describe the liquid that is obtained by infusion, this is called the liqueur.

• **Liqueur:** see above.

• **In the mouth:** the group of characteristics perceived in the mouth, comprising smell, touch and taste.

• **In the nose:** see bouquet.

• **Scent:** smell.

• **Smell:** perceived directly by the nose, as opposed to the aromas that are felt in the mouth.

Description of tea tasting (flavour and texture)

• **Aromatic:** this is said of a liqueur that is strong and high in flavour.

• **Astringent:** having a rather harsh and rough quality in the mouth, caused by tannins.

• **Biting:** this denotes a tea which is both astringent and sour and that leaves a strong and lasting impression.

• **Bitter:** one of the five flavours. Normal for some teas that are high in tannin. Bitterness has the tendency to develop if the tea is left to infuse for too long.

• **Body:** characteristic of a beverage that marries a good constitution (robust) with warm aromas.

• **Complex:** this denotes a very rich mix of aromas, of great subtlety.

• **Creamy:** see mellow.

• **Delicacy:** the quality of a delicate liqueur with many, subtle aromas.

• **Flavourful:** this is said of a liqueur with strong, rich flavours.

• **Flowing:** denotes a smooth, pleasant beverage, with no harshness. Used to refer to teas with a low tannin content.

• **Frank:** this denotes teas whose characteristics (colour, scent, flavours, aromas...) are well defined and express themselves unfailingly and without ambiguity.

• **Fresh:** this is said of slightly sour teas that give a feeling of freshness.

• **Frivolous:** this is said of teas that are both rich in aromas and short in the mouth. They give a feeling of fleetingness.

• **Full in the mouth:** giving a very pleasant sensation and filling the mouth well. See also round.

• **Full-bodied:** said of a beverage that has body.

• **Generous:** rich in aromas, while not being tiring, which can be the case with heady teas.

• **Glutinous:** one of the five flavours, never found in tea. It can be detected above all in a majority of Asian dishes since it is associated with the presence of glutamates in food.

TEA TASTING

- **Greenness:** a fresh and green quality.
- **Harsh:** a biting sensation, a little rough, caused by tannins.
- **Heady:** this is said of a beverage that is high in spicy and flowery aromas.
- **Invigorating:** a characteristic of young, green tea, where there is a pronounced sour note.
- **Iodised:** a note found in certain teas such as Japanese green teas.
- **Light:** this is said of a tea that is not very full-bodied, with a low tannin content.
- **Lively:** this is said of a tea whose characteristics are well defined, with a slight hint of sourness.
- **Long in the mouth:** this is said of a tea in which the

aromas leave a pleasant and long-lasting impression in the front and the back of the mouth after tasting.
- **Mellow:** this is said of a tea that is both round in the mouth and slightly sour. See also creamy, silky.
- **Mild:** this is said of beverages whose flavour is slightly sweet, punctured perhaps by a hint of acidity, but which have no astringency. See mellow, velvety, silky.
- **Odorous:** this is said of a beverage or an infusion with many strong scents.
- **Pointed:** see sharp.
- **Powerful:** denotes a full-bodied, long-lasting liqueur.
- **Raw:** green and sourer than the average.
- **Refined:** this is said of a tea whose scents, flavours and aromas are both delicate and subtle.
- **Robust:** this is said of a predominantly tannic beverage, which fills the mouth well. See round, full.
- **Rough:** this is said of a tea that is very astringent, often of bad quality or else has been infused for far too long.
- **Round:** this is said of a liqueur in which the smoothness and mellowness give an impression of roundness in the mouth.
- **Roundness:** the quality of a liqueur that fills the mouth in a spherical way.
- **Salted:** one of the five senses. Non-existent in

tea that contains absolutely no sodium.
- **Sharp:** this is used to refer to a very lively beverage, in which there is an obvious fresh and sour note, almost spicy, and in which each aroma is delicately expressed.
- **Short in the mouth:** leaving few traces in the front or the back of the mouth after tasting.
- **Silky:** this denotes a smooth and mellow tea, with a touch of harmony, bringing to mind the smoothness of silk.
- **Slippery:** see flowing.
- **Smooth:** denotes a beverage without harshness, owing to the lack of tannins. See slippery, flowing.
- **Sour:** this is one of the five flavours. It is found in some green teas, Wu Long (oolong) and spring Darjeeling, to which it gives freshness and liveliness.
- **Strong:** a rather vague term, which usually denotes a full-bodied, highly coloured liqueur.
- **Sturdy:** denotes a tea whose constitution is very robust. A quality that can be softened with milk.
- **Subtle:** this denotes a tea with delicate and complex scents and aromas.
- **Supple:** this is said of a liqueur where the mellowness overcomes the astringency. See slippery, flowing.
- **Sustained:** this denotes an aroma that stays in the

mouth for a long time.

- **Sweet:** one of the five flavours, which can be detected sometimes in certain very light, green teas from China. Rather rare, except in Ama Cha tea.
- **Tannic:** this is said of a liqueur with a high tannin content.
- **Umami:** one of the five tastes. It can be identified in many examples of Asian cuisine, since it is linked to the presence of glutamate in foodstuffs.
- **Velvety:** this is said of a smooth, velvety liqueur, almost sweet.
- **Vigorous:** this is said of a tea that is both astringent and lively, whose presence is immediately felt in the mouth.
- **Vivacious:** this is said of a fresh, light beverage with a hint of sourness that is slightly, but not excessively, dominant. All in all very pleasant.
- **Voluptuous:** used to refer to a beverage that is full, round and long-lasting in the mouth.
- **Warm:** denotes spicy, woody aromas married to flavour that is totally lacking in acidity; by extension it is used to describe beverages having these qualities.
- **Young:** this denotes teas that were plucked early and which have a green, slightly sour character.

Olfactory and retro-olfactory characteristics (scents, aromas)

Here is a list of terms commonly used to describe the olfactory and retro-olfactory impressions that occur during tea tasting and that allow us to express these sensations with reference to known aromas.

Hesperian notes:
These refer to citrus fruit aromas.
Lemony
Orangey
Zesty

Fruity notes:
Bitter almond
Black fruit
Dried fruit
Fruity
Green almond
Green apple
Muscat grape
Peach
Red fruit
Ripe fruit
Ripe grape

Floral notes:
All flowery notes and in particular:
Freesia
Iris
Jasmine
Narcissus
Orchid
Rose

Spicy notes:
Aniseed
Cocoa
Honey
Liquorice
Malt
Menthol
Nutmeg
Pepper

Vegetable and Woodland notes:
These are the woody, balsamic, musty notes.
Bark
Chestnut
Damp earth after a storm
Dry wood
Green wood
Herb
Moss
Peat
Rocky
Undergrowth
Woody

Empyreal notes:
Denoting a series of aromas and smells which bring to mind smoke, burning, caramelising.
Burnt
Grilled
Smoked

How to use the tea guide?

O n the following pages we would like to introduce you to all the teas and scented blends chosen or created by Le Palais des Thés. Packed with valuable information and practical tips, this guide will enable you to thoroughly know and skillfully select the teas you wish to sample.

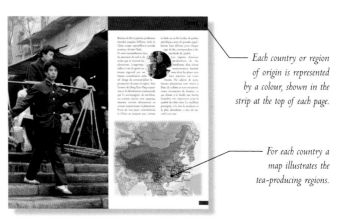

Each country or region of origin is represented by a colour, shown in the strip at the top of each page.

For each country a map illustrates the tea-producing regions.

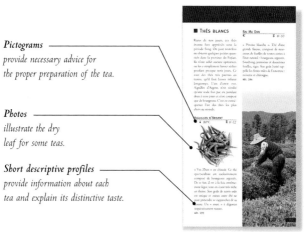

Pictograms — provide necessary advice for the proper preparation of the tea.

Photos illustrate the dry leaf for some teas.

Short descriptive profiles — provide information about each tea and explain its distinctive taste.

Key to the symbols used

perfect in the morning	all day long	perfect in the evening	infusion temperature	infusion time

Key to colour code

Our buying policy

ASIA

China, Taiwan,
Indonesia, Vietnam,
Malaysia

ASIA

Japan

ASIA

India, Sri Lanka, Nepal,
Bangladesh

FROM THE BLACK SEA
TO THE CASPIAN SEA

Iran, Turkey, Georgia

AFRICA

Rwanda, Cameroon,
Kenya, Mauritius,
Zimbabwe

SOUTH AMERICA

Argentina

BLENDS AND FLAVOURS

Traditional English
blends, Russian blends,
Flowers from China,
Scented blends

CERTIFIED
ORGANIC
TEAS

Ever since the founding of Le Palais des Thés we have decided to buy direct from the plantations. Every year, therefore, our experts travel in about 20 countries, mostly in Asia but also in Africa and South America.

The fact that we travel so extensively, that we taste and buy on location has many advantages and allows us in particular:

- *to find rare crops by looking outside the traditional supplier circuit, to taste and to share with you the harvests of small plantations, which are often so hidden away that their production is almost exclusively sold in local markets,*

- *to guarantee regular quality control of the teas we buy and to periodically check up on the plucking methods, the way they are worked, and treated in their actual place of manufacture.*

- *to get to know the planters together with their way of running their plantations, requiring from them that they operate in accordance with our buying code of ethics, that is to say:*
  - *no child or forced labour,*
  - *respect for the environment and adoption of clean farming methods,*
  - *no deforestation,*
  - *decent salaries for the workers,*
  - *compliance with health and safety regulations,*

- *to establish lasting relationships, based on trust and friendship with our suppliers, an essential condition for the success of any business.*

China was the birthplace of tea and the primary world supplier until the 19th century; it now stands second, behind India. Plantations are mainly found in the southern and central provinces. For a long time they were managed on a regional level by an exclusive central body, which was responsible for selling the whole region's production. When Deng Xiao Ping came to power, there was a liberalisation of trade and consequently many private companies were born bringing the plantations and the importers into direct contact with each other. Strengthened by its centralised past China does not, as does India or Sri Lanka, offer us the products of specific plantations but rather proposes large, well-defined 'denominations' for each type of tea, relating to different qualities.

The tea-producing regions of China have a moderate wet climate in which the rainfall is evenly distributed throughout the year. On the other hand, many plantations are situated on the hillsides with very constant low clouds, giving the leaves a high moisture content, a very important factor to the quality of green teas. The main harvest, which is both the best and the most important, takes place from mid April to mid May.

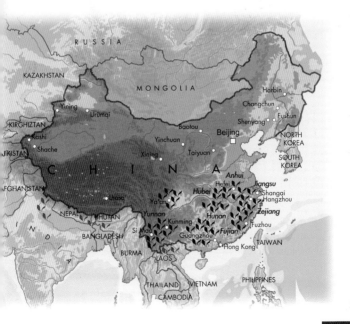

■ OFFERING THE BEST

Quality standards apply mainly to black teas, essentially reserved for export and produced on a very large scale, making it even easier to have a consistent quality, by blending many batches. As for green teas, especially the most prestigious ones, these are often produced in much smaller quantities, which makes them rare. It is sometimes not an easy task to reach the same quality from one year to the next.

Huang Hua Yun Jian

In order to appreciate all their delicacy and freshness, these green teas should be drunk while they are still 'new season', in other words in the eight to ten months following the harvest. This is why Le Palais des Thés has decided to adopt the same buying policy for these green teas denominations as the ones we use for spring Darjeelings. So every year our experts visit plantations in Anhui, Fujian, Zhejiang, Yunnan, Jiangsu or Sichuan to select the best teas of the moment and send them to France as quickly as possible.

Huang Shan Mao Feng

Xue Ya

Yi Go Mao Jian

This selection, renewed every year, is usually available from June onwards, with the exception of air freighted teas that are sold from May, just a few weeks after the leaves were plucked.

Yu Huan

Five famous new season teas

◼ WHITE TEAS

Although rare nowadays, these teas were greatly appreciated during the Song dynasty. We can however still get some of it in small quantities in the Fujian province. The leaves have not undergone any process: they have simply been allowed to dry for almost three days. These teas have a very low tannin content and they need to be brewed for a long time. One of them, *Aiguilles d'Argent* made up entirely of buds, is plucked once a year over a two to three days period. This explains why it is one of the most expensive teas in the world.

AIGUILLES D'ARGENT
◆ ♨ 160°F   ⧖ 8'-12'

Silver Needles or 'Yin Zhen' in Chinese. This spectacular tea is exclusively made up of silvery buds, that's why it is extremely light. Its ripe grape taste is unique and no other tea can come even closer to its delicacy. Drinking it with nothing added is an absolute must.

REF. 193

BAI MU DAN
☽ ♨ 180°F   ⧖ 8'-10'

'White peony'. A very fine tea, made up of all sorts of leaves in their natural state: silvery buds, Souchong leaves, first and second leaves and stems. It's woody taste is like the autumn fruit: hazelnuts and chestnuts. PHOTO P. 15

REF. 194

■ GREEN TEAS

Green tea, the daily drink of the Chinese people, accounts for 80% of the total production with a large part reserved for home consumption. It is mainly grown in the mountainous, humid regions of Anhui, Zhejiang, Jiangsu, Fujian and Guanxi. The leaves can be folded, twisted, rolled lengthwise (needles), or made into balls or other shapes. These teas are known by their freshness, their greenness and their long lasting flavour in the mouth. As a general rule, they should be infused for three minutes.

Le Palais des Thés offers:
● about ten very prestigious teas yearly, chosen from amongst hundreds of exclusive teas produced in China in small quantities. Extremely fresh and of an exceptional delicacy they are replaced from year to year in line with new recommendations and should, for maximum enjoyment, be consumed new season, within eight to ten months of plucking.
● the teas with the constant best reputation in China.

■ new season green teas
please refer to the price list for this year

■ folded leaves
This type of manual treatment of the leaf produces a mild and velvety tea.

LONG JING
☀ 🌡 180°F   ⧖ 3'

'Dragon's well' is one of the best known Chinese teas. It originates from the Zhejiang province and grows at the top of the Tian Mu Mountains. It is recognized by its fold which copy the shape of the original leaf. It has a delicate perfume, a slightly sweet and silky taste. A velvety liqueur, long lasting taste in the mouth with a chestnut scent. It is a good introduction to green tea.

LOOSE: REF. 198

IN A TIN (100G): REF. DVN198

IN MUSLIN TEA BAGS: REF. D198S

PING CHA
☀ 🌡 180°F   ⧖ 3'

Literally, 'Flat tea', from the province of Zhejiang. This is the Chinese people everyday tea, mild and fresh.

REF. 199

■ twisted leaves

A twisted leaf usually gives a delicate, scented tea, a little more full bodied than teas from folded leaves.

GU ZHANG MAO JIAN

☀ 🌡 180°F ⏳ 4'

A subtle, high-growing tea, which has the scent of damp soil after a storm, which the Chinese particularly enjoy. Lightly full-bodied.

REF. 209

LONG ZHU

☀ 🌡 180°F ⏳ 4'

Round, delicate and scented, this tea develops the same woody notes as Gu Zhang Mao Jian but without any sharpness.

REF. 210

LIN YUN

☀ 🌡 180°F ⏳ 4'

A tea with a pronounced scent and a thirst quenching taste.

REF. 211

CHUN MEI

☀ 🌡 180°F ⏳ 4'

'Old man's eyebrow'. A tea rolled into needles that develops a pleasing aroma of fresh leaves. Powerful and scented.

REF. 213

GUNPOWDER

☀ 🌡 180°F ⏳ 4'

This tea is rolled into little pearls, used for the traditional preparation of Moroccan mint tea. Lively and astringent, fresh and thirst quenching.

REF. 214

■ rolled leaves

In this case the tea is more invigorating and more astringent because of the way the leaf is fashioned.

Red Huan cup
Ref. N006A

Beige Huan cup
Ref. N006B

Blue Huan cup
Ref. N006C

■ Wu Long or semi fermented teas

These also include the teas that the Chinese call blue-green. The teas, which have long, pale leaves before treatment, are processed using three types of fermentation:

- a light fermentation (10%-15%) that the Chinese call 'Wu-Yi' after the name of the mountains in the Fujian province where the teas grow,
- an intermediate fermentation (30%-40%), which produces among others the Tie Guan Yin teas,
- a stronger fermentation (50%-60%), with a resemblance to the Wu Long (oolong) teas from Taiwan.

These are perfect in the late afternoon or evening. They are highly regarded by traditional Chinese medicine: they are thirst quenching, calming and help the digestion of fatty foods. Wu Long (oolong) teas can be prepared in a traditional teapot, using 0,4 to 0,7oz of tea per litre of water and allowing it to infuse for 7 to 8 minutes. They can also be enjoyed using the Gong Fu Cha method (page 56) in tiny teapots that are filled with leaves and allowed to infuse for 30 to 60 seconds. Very high quality semi fermented teas can be infused several times without spoiling the taste.

■ light fermentation (10%-15%)

GRAND SHUI XIAN
☾ ♨ 205°F   ⏳ 5'-7'
'Narcissus or Water Fairy'. A thirst quenching tea from the Fujian province. Its taste is fresh and iodised. Exceptionally mild.

REF. 2175

■ intermediate fermentation (30%-40%)

TIE GUAN YIN IMPÉRIAL
☾ ♨ 205°F   ⏳ 5'-7'

'Iron Goddess of Mercy'. This is the highest quality Tie Guan Yin tea. The leaves are almost black dark green, with a slightly yellow tint around the edges. It produces an amber liqueur with a hazelnut-like, flowery bouquet. Long lasting taste in the mouth, this is a tea of great delicacy.

REF. 2165

Tie Guan Yin

☾ 🌡 205°F   ⏳ 5'-7'

The darkest and the most woody of the semi fermented teas from China. A beautiful amber infusion, which evokes cinnamon and liquorice. It is the Chinese's favourite tea.

REF. 217

■ stronger fermentation (50%-60%)

Kuai

☾ 🌡 205°F   ⏳ 5'-7'

The most scented and the most flowery, this semi fermented tea is enlivened by the addition of cinnamon flower pollen and orchid pistils.

REF. 216

■ Black teas

The birth of black tea in China is very mysterious. No one knows exactly what lead the Chinese to start fermenting tea after having produced only green tea for centuries. One legend says that black tea was the accidental result of a cargo of green tea having fermented during an overly long sea crossing. Having arrived at its destination the tea was greatly appreciated by its recipients, who then went on to order some more… Whatever the case, black teas are essentially produced for export. They come from the Yunnan, Anhui, Fujian, Jiangxi and Sichuan regions.

■ Yunnan

This is a high altitude tea, which produces a highly coloured infusion. It is a round, full tea with no bitterness and a long lasting flavour. It is considered one of the best black teas in the world. Its honey taste is unique. This tea enjoys great success, since it mixes the two characteristics that many tea drinkers seek: a light, mild tea that is, at the same time, full-bodied and long lasting in the mouth. These qualities make it, perhaps, the ideal tea to start with should one wish to make the switch from coffee to tea.

BOURGEONS DE YUNNAN
☀ 🌡 205°F   ⏳ 3'-5'

'Yunnan buds' are a spectacular and exceptional crop. Made up almost exclusively of very long, golden buds, this tea is to black tea what *Aiguilles d'Argent* are to white tea: the very essence of delicacy, which delights tea lovers. On being infused, the leaf releases a strong, deep scent, with earthy, almost animal, notes reminiscent of truffles. The liqueur is dark, almost black and its full and generous bouquet evokes cocoa. Without question, the best of the Yunnan teas.

REF. 2185

YUNNAN D'OR
☀ 🌡 205°F   ⏳ 3'-5'

'Golden Yunnan' is an exceptional crop of a rare delicacy that Le Palais des Thés experts source directly from the plantations, something which is very difficult in China because the marketing of tea is still very centralized on a regional basis. This is one of the finest, the most delicate and the most subtle of the Yunnan teas. PHOTO P. 21.

REF. 219

GRAND YUNNAN IMPÉRIAL

☀ 🌡 205°F   ⏳ 3'-5'

The great character and subtlety of this tea, both flowery and mild, has earned it the name of 'the Mocha of teas' or 'the Surgeons' tea' since it wakes one up without making one nervous. It has magnificent leaves with many golden buds and gives a highly coloured beverage. A wonderful morning tea with a honey scent.

LOOSE: REF. 220

IN A TIN (100G): REF. DVN220

IN MUSLIN BAGS: REF. D220S

4 oz tea canister of Thé des Songes:
Ref. DV896A
Empty tin:
Ref. V401A

GRAND YUNNAN

☀ 🌡 205°F   ⏳ 3'-5'

Mild, with plenty of character.

REF. 221

■ Qimen

Qimen teas are grown in a low-lying region in the province of Anhui, west of Shanghai. They are very light, very fine teas that can be drunk at the end of the day. The leaves are short, tightly rolled and very black. The beverage has a cocoa flavour.

A WORD FROM AN EXPERT: XU HE

Tea export manager for the Province of Yunnan

'With Le Palais des Thés, I am dealing with real enthusiasts, their experts are always on the look out for new teas, for finer crops: this fact is well known in the Yunnan province and I regularly get small producers coming to see me to introduce teas they wish to grow especially for Le Palais des Thés. This was the case, for example, with the Bourgeons de Yunnan…'

'If there is one thing I really appreciate with Le Palais des Thés team, apart from the many years of friendship that bind us, it is their ability to pass on their passion and to introduce their customers to the teas they have discovered. The case of Grand Yunnan Impérial is typical: we did not sell this tea in France fifteen years ago. Le Palais des Thés began to introduce it to its customers and it has become a very big seller for us: today Le Palais des Thés is our most important customer for this quality of Yunnan tea.'

QIMEN IMPÉRIAL

☀ 🌡 205°F   ⏳ 3'-5'

This is the best quality Qimen tea that exists. It is a extremely hard to find: one of the rarest and most sought after in the Anhui province. Deliberately produced in small quantities, Qimen Impérial owes its fame to its leathery flavour and its unique malty taste.

REF. 223

Qimen Hao Ya
☀ 🌡 205°F   ⏳ 3'-5'
Like the previous tea, this tea grows on the Huang Mountain. It is a high quality crop. The tea has a delicate, slightly chocolaty, taste. A subtle tea for the late afternoon.
REF. 224

Qimen Da Bie
☀ 🌡 205°F   ⏳ 3'-5'
A fine and delicate tea that grows on the Da Bie Mountain. A good introduction to Qimen teas.
REF. 2245

Qimen
☀ 🌡 205°F   ⏳ 3'-5'
For daytime drinking.
REF. 225

In the interests of authenticity, we respect the Chinese denominations of origin and for this reason we use the official spellings known as PIN YIN:

Chun Mee: Chun Mei
Chung Feng: Chun Feng
Keemun: Qimen
Kwai: Kuai
Long Zhong: Long Zhu
Lung Ching: Long Jing
Oolong: Wu Long
Pai Mu Tan: Bai Mu Dan
Pu Ehr: Pu Er
Se Chung: Se Zhong
Shui Hsien: Shui Xian
Tieh Kuan Yin: Tie Guan Yin

■ SMOKED TEAS

Produced in the Fujian province, these teas are obtained from Souchong leaves (low, large sized leaves), which are smoked with spruce tree roots. They are suitable for any time of day and can be drunk with meals or savoury breakfasts.

Grand Lapsang Souchong
☾ 🌡 205°F   ⏳ 4'-5'
The finest and the lightest of the smoked teas. Its delicate flavour is easy to distinguish with its two components: a tea taste and smoked notes. PHOTO P. 15
REF. 240

Pointes Blanches
☾ 🌡 205°F　　　　⏳ 4'-5'
A great classic among teas. Flowery with silvery buds.
REF. 241

Lapsang Souchong
☾ 🌡 205°F　　　　⏳ 4'-5'
More smoked than the previous two teas.
REF. 242

■ YELLOW TEAS

Produced very irregularly, these are extremely rare teas which Le Palais des Thés is able to buy some years. When this happens the teas are introduced together with the list of new season green teas.

■ DARK TEAS

These teas come from Yunnan province and are being fermented in heaps under a damp cover, in order to maintain a degree of hygrometry greater than 85%. The dark teas are usually put through this process several times.

These dark teas, or Pu Ers, improve with age, and the older teas sometimes command higher prices at auction.

■ whole leaves

Pu Er Impérial
☀ 🌡 205°F　　　　⏳ 4'

A very fine crop, with many buds. Its powerful scent is reminiscent of damp soil and bark. Its name means 'trouser bottom'. A Chinese folk tale tells how the tea pickers keep the best leaves for themselves, hiding them in their pockets before taking them home with them.

Pu Er tea is highly regarded in Chinese medicine for its curative properties. '*It lowers cholesterol levels, they say, it dissolves fats, helps digestion, improves blood circulation and lowers the effects of alcohol.*'

This tea improves with age, owing to the specific type of oxidation that affects the tannins.

LOOSE: REF. 215

IN A TIN (100G): REF. DVN215

IN MUSLIN TEAS BAGS: REF. D215S

Imperial yellow bowl – Ref. N020

■ compressed dark teas

These teas represent an ancient way of drinking tea. This type of tea was used to pay tithes in feudal China and was compressed into different shapes for easier transport. They were mostly Pu Er teas.

QI ZI BING CHA
☾ ☌ 205°F   ⧗ 4'

Round cake of Pu Er tea from the Xishuangbanna region in the Yunnan province. Presented in its original packaging, it consists of several compressed layers of black Pu Er.
REF. C281

TEA BRAID
⧗ 4'

This is a braid of dried banana leaves encircling five balls of compressed tea, which can be used as a tincture or in the bath water, to aid relaxation.
REF. C285

For more information about the teas and traditions of China we recommend you read Thé et Tao *(in French) by John Blofeld, Albin Michel, Paris 1997. Ref. L007.*

CINNAMON WOOD TEA

In the village of Jinhong located in the heart of the Golden Triangle, between China and Laos, an ancestral tradition is kept alive. When the new moon signals the start of the New Year, the young adults of the village offer the famous tea of the Pu Er mountains, known for its long-life-giving qualities, to their elders.

In the days leading up to the festival, they go off into the forest to find a cinnamon tree and fashion a box from one of its branches in which they collect the precious tea. After having been kept for several days, the leaves are mixed with a subtle aroma of cinnamon.

Cinnamon wood tea - Ref. D015

■ THAILAND

Tea was first grown in Thailand in the 1980s by a Chinese commu- nity in Mae Salong, in the north of the country. Using plants and tech- niques from Taiwan, some very high quality semi-oxidised teas are now grown in Thailand.

GAN NEN
☾ 🌡 205°F   ⏳ 7'

Gan Nen is a light semi-oxidised tea (30%) with fresh, fruity and slightly woody aromas.
REF. 310

MILKY WU LONG
☾ 🌡 205°F   ⏳ 7'

A superb tea from the Jin Xuan cultivar, famous for its buttery, vanilla fragrance.
RÉF. 315

■ INDONESIA

JAVA MALABAR O.P.
☀ 🌡 205°F   ⏳ 3'-5'
A good Orange Pekoe, which can be drunk all day.
REF. 320

■ VIETNAM

VIETNAM F.B.O.P.
☀ 🌡 205°F   ⏳ 2'-5'
Broken, flowery and lightly full-bodied.
REF. 330

■ MALAYSIA

MALAISIE O.P.
☀ 🌡 205°F   ⏳ 3'-5'
To be drunk all day.
REF. 335

The island of Taiwan still bears its old name of Formosa when it comes to tea. Annexed by the Chinese at the end of the 17ᵗʰ century, Formosa began producing tea in very small quantities from plants that had been transplanted from the province of Fujian. It was only with the coming to power of the communists in 1949 that production was considerably increased and diversified. The island is extremely fertile and possesses ideal growing conditions: high altitude plantations with a constant temperature of 54°F-68°F and good humidity. Taiwan is well known for its semi fermented teas called 'Wu Long (oolong)', also

called 'Black Dragon' in Chinese. These teas can undergo various levels of fermentation depending on the plantation, something that makes it rather pointless to compare Chinese with Taiwanese methods. It is the Taiwanese that have long prevailed in the classification of Wu Long (oolong) teas.

Taiwanese teas are therefore classified according to their degree of fermentation and not to their method of production.

Taiwan makes both green and black, of which the famous Tarry Souchong smoked teas are renowned for their unusual strength.

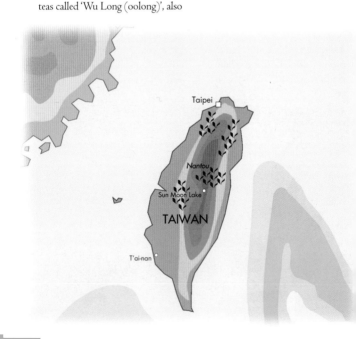

■ SEMI FERMENTED TEAS

■ light fermentation: 10%-15%

BAO ZHONG IMPÉRIAL

☾ ☷ 205°F　　　　　**⧗ 5'-7'**

This is one of the most celebrated teas from Taiwan. Its Chinese name is 'wrapped in paper' and reminds us that this tea, before fermentation, is wrapped in a white sheet of cotton paper to preserve the delicacy of its leaves. A very beautiful tea with large, twisted leaves that produces a pale yellow beverage, with a flowery, almost peppery taste that evokes narcissus and jasmine flowers that majestically associate greenness and mildness.

REF. 265

ORGANIC TEAS

Le Palais des Thés offers a selection of teas that have been organically grown. These teas can change from one year to the next. Please refer to the price list for the year in progress.

Donf Ding - ref. 264

■ intermediate fermentation: 30%-40%

DONG DING
☾ ☷ 205°F   ⌛ 5'-7'

This tea which grows on the eponymous mountain, means 'Icy peak'. It is considered by tea lovers to be one of Taiwan's best. The leaf, which is pearly and moderately fermented, gives the liqueur a particular yellow-orange colour that is unique in the world of tea. Its scent is both silky and lively, its taste recalls the flowery side of the little fermented 'Wu Long' (oolong) teas and also that of the fruitier, woodier Fancy teas. An exceptional crop. PHOTO P. 15. REF. 264

■ very heavy fermentation: 70% and over

It is this type of fermentation in particular that has led to the fame of Taiwanese teas and it was to these teas that the name 'Wu Long (oolong)' was originally given. They are easily recognised by their brown colour and by the size of their leaves. They have a woody taste that is reminiscent of hazelnut and chestnut.

GRAND WU LONG TOP FANCY
☾ ☷ 205°F   ⌛ 5'-7'

The most famous of the 'Black Dragon' teas. Plucked in spring, it has a high concentration of buds, the ripe grape flavour marries remarkably well with the dark, woody flavour of the lower leaves. Of very great subtlety, it is imperative that this tea be prepared under perfect conditions according to the rules of Gong Fu Cha if its full delicacy is to be expressed. REF. 260

China, Taiwan and Vietnam Gift box.
12 tubes of tea from these three countries- Ref. DCMCE

In the interests of authenticity, we respect the Chinese denominations of origin and for this reason we use the official spellings known as PIN YIN:

Oolong: Wu Long
Tung Ting: Dong Ding
Pouchong: Bao Zhong

BUTTERFLY OF TAIWAN

☾ 🌡 205°F   ⏳ 5'-7'

A superb tea, delicate and scented. All the qualities of Wu Long (oolong) teas are well defined in this tea: it is woody and honeyed, round and long lasting in the mouth. This is the tea to sample first when discovering these typical Taiwanese teas. It must be drunk alone, with nothing added.

REF. 267

FANCY

☾ 🌡 205°F   ⏳ 5'-7'

A very good Wu Long (oolong), dark and subtle. Stronger than the previous tea.

REF. 261

CHOICEST

☾ 🌡 205°F   ⏳ 5'-7'

Mild and aromatic. Equally good in a blend as a means of softening a black tea.

REF. 262

■ SMOKED BLACK TEAS

THÉ DU TIGRE

☾ 🌡 205°F   ⏳ 4'-5'

'Tiger Tea'. This is the tea that, because of its strength, has given Taiwanese smoked teas their reputation. The leaf is superb and the smoking process is carried out in accordance with the rules of the craft: many long hours over a fire made from spruce roots. This is certainly one of the most smoked of the smokey teas and is also one of the favourites of tea lovers.

LOOSE: REF. 271

IN A TIN (100G): REF. DVN271

IN MUSLIN BAGS: REF. D271S

TARRY LAPSANG SOUCHONG

☾ 🌡 205°F   ⏳ 4'-5'

Less smoked than the *Thé du Tigre*, this is nonetheless still stronger than all the Chinese Lapsang Souchong teas.

REF. 270

I n their everyday lives, the Chinese do not use a teapot, but prepare their tea in small individual bowls – zhong bowls – into which they place a little green tea and then pour on boiling water. The bowl is covered with a special lid that allows the tea to be drunk without swallowing the leaves. Tea drinkers will continue to re-infuse the same leaves many times throughout the day and will take their bowls with them wherever they go.

Alongside this everyday form of tea drinking, there is the Chinese tradition of tea drinking, Gong Fu Cha, which has been adopted in Taiwan for several decades now.

It was during the Ming dynasty that the practice of infusing tea first became widespread, that the first teapots appeared and that Yi Xing clay began to be used in their production. Tea drinking at the time was a refined and social act, which aimed to recapture and to imitate the forgotten rituals of the Song tradition. This aim led to the creation of a tea manual, the *Cha Shu*, which described in great detail every step in the preparation of tea and on which the Taiwanese Gong Fu Cha is directly based.

Today its set of rules are observed in most Taiwanese teahouses, where tea lovers can get together in a warm and friendly environment.

The teas drunk there are of an exceptional quality, most often they are Wu Long (oolong) with very delicate aromas and long lasting flavours, that require teapots made from a particular type of clay: clay from Yi Xing, a Chinese village to the west of Shanghai (see page 58). Amongst other accessories one typically finds: the kettle; the tea boat, a sort of large shallow dish onto which the teapot and cups are placed; the spare pot, the smelling and the tasting cups.

So how is tea prepared according to Gong Fu Cha?
• place the teapot and the cups on the tea boat,
• pour some hot water into the teapot to rinse it and then pour this water away into the spare pot,
• put enough tea leaves into the teapot to half fill it. Rinse the leaves with a little water just to moisten them, then immediately pour the rinsing water into the spare pot,
• pour the contents of this pot into the tea boat,

DISCOVER THE ART OF GONG FU CHA WITH THE TEA SCHOOL

GO FURTHER WITH L'ÉCOLE DU THÉ

• fill the teapot with water to the top as to force out any scum. Leave to infuse for one minute and then pour the liqueur into the spare pot,
• fill the smelling cup from the pot and then immediately transfer its contents into the tasting cup.
The tea lover inhales deeply from the first cup in order to take in the scent of the tea and then drinks from the second cup, savouring it slowly and taking little sips. The infusion is repeated several times following the same procedure.

Tea prepared in this way is much stronger than ordinary tea; it should be savoured like a liqueur and taken in very small quantities. Every artefact used, each gesture performed, has the aim of drawing out and extracting the scents and the aromas of the tea, which makes Gong Fu Cha primarily an art of tea tasting.

Y i Xing is a Chinese town situated in the south of Jiangsu province about three hours by train from Shanghai. It is very famous for its exceptional clay, which the Chinese commonly refer to as 'purple clay' owing to the purplish brown colour it develops when heated.

Today 70% of the town's economic activity is linked to the extraction and the fashioning of this clay, especially into teapots. Yi Xing clay has a particularly high level of iron and silicon, which gives it interesting properties and makes it clearly superior to other clays in the manufacture of a good teapot:

● firstly, it hardly shrinks hence preventing objects becoming formed during heating and allowing the teapots to be fashioned into controlled and regular shapes,

● secondly, it has great porosity, excellent for the oxygenation of the tea and allows a better diffusion of the aromas than in any other receptacle,

● lastly, Yi Xing clay, unlike most clays, is not grainy and as a result transmits heat less quickly than other clays: a Yi Xing teapot will not burn your hands and will not break when it goes from cold to hot.

It was under the Ming dynasty (1368–1644) that the Chinese started to use this clay to manufacture teapots, at the same time that the practice of infusing tea became popular. Teapots have always inspired the greatest artists as they represent a window

Red Huan teapot
Re. M102

Beige Huan teapot
Ref. M103

Blue Huan teapot
Ref. M104

for the skilful craft of the potters of Yi Xing. In the beginning they were all very large (about one litre capacity), but it was realised that small teapots were better for conserving and releasing the scent of tea; this explains why some Yi Xing teapots only contain the equivalent of one or two cups of tea.

In China it is traditionally Wu Long (oolong) teas, more rarely black or green teas, that are infused in Yi Xing teapots. The Japanese, who are the biggest buyers of these teapots, reserve them for the best Sencha teas.

Several rules have to be followed to prepare tea in a Yi Xing teapot:
• do not infuse too many different types of tea in the same teapot: a strong tea will leave a persistent taste that will mask that of subsequent teas, if they are less strong,
• the first tea is reserved for the teapot itself: a teapot that has never been used will absorb a lot during the first infusion, it becomes seasoned. The clay will affect the taste of this first infusion; it is therefore preferable not to drink it but to offer it to the teapot,
• above all never use detergents of any sort; the teapot would absorb their flavour.
A simple rinse with clear water between teas is the best.

Tea appeared in Japan under the influence of the Chinese Tang dynasty, during the 7th century, but its widespread adoption by Japanese society was very slow. For a long time, tea was a privilege reserved for the priests, being drunk only by Zen Buddhist monks. It was not until the 9th century that the first tea plants were grown, and not until 1202 that they were planted in the province of Uji, which is now famed for producing the best green teas in Japan. Later the great Zen priest, Sen-no Rikyu (1522-1591) classified the link between tea, Buddhism and the different schools of tea, creating in this way to the most complete form of Cha No Yu. To the exception of the Matcha tea ceremony, Japan today produces many whole leaf green teas of very high quality whose preparation demands some special cares. The delicacy of the leaf requires a quick infusion and a water temperature which is lower the higher the quality of tea.

JAPAN

Unlike all the other green teas produced in the world, Japanese green teas are not prepared according to the traditional Chinese process, as described on page 14, but undergo a special type of firing, by using steam. The leaves, instead of being roasted in a boiling hot receptacle, are steamed for a few minutes, which gives them a shiny appearance and a slightly iodised taste which is immediately recognizable.

Because of this typical appearance and flavour, Japanese green teas often provoke surprise in Westerners. They must be drunk unadulterated, with nothing added.

GYOKURO

Gyokuro teas are the most prestigious green teas of Japan and are some of the most expensive teas in the world. They are only plucked once a year, and only in selected plantations. A few weeks before the harvest, the planter takes care to cover the tea plants with sheets or with bamboo straw matting, to filter 90% of the sun's rays. Starved of light, the tealeaf softens and starts producing much more chlorophyll than it would have done in the open air, which gives the tea a flavour of incomparable freshness and purity.

GYOKURO HIKARI

☀ 🌡 120°F   ⧗ 2'-2'30"

'Pearl of Dew'. One of the best Gyokuro teas from the province of Uji. To create this exceptional tea the tenderest buds are selected by hand, something that is very rare in Japan, and then one by one, finely rolled. In this tea one discovers a lively, fresh taste, with an absolute remarkable delicacy and roundness; the result of a refinement and a degree of care that only the Japanese are capable of. A tea to delight any tea lover.
For optimum enjoyment infuse 0,35 oz of tea in 60ml of water at 120°F for two minutes.

PHOTO P. 15.

REF. 300

62

MATCHA IMPÉRIAL

☀ 🌡 180°F   ⧗ 30"

'Mousse of Liquid Jade'. This is also a Gyokuro tea, in this case ground with a millstone to a very fine powder, which is mainly destined for the Japanese tea ceremony: Cha No Yu. The tea is beaten with a whisk in a bowl and not infused in a teapot. Invigorating and strong, Matcha Impérial is usually taken immediately after a very sweet dish for a full enjoyment of its subtle bitterness. Tasting recommendations: 0,05 oz of tea in 40ml of water at 180°F. Whisk the mixture vigorously for 30 seconds until a frothy liquid is obtained and drink immediately.

REF. C230

▨ SENCHA

Sencha teas are green teas very widespread in Japan. Their name in Japanese means 'infused tea'. They are produced several times a year using the best leaves from the tea plants. The plucking is done mechanically, a technique that the Japanese have mastered so they can obtain teas of different grades. After steam firing, the leaves are folded to look like small flat needles. A Sencha tea is prepared with varying quantities of tea, differing volumes and temperatures of water, as well as different times of infusion, depending on its quality.

RYOKUCHA MIDORI

☀ 🌡 140°F   ⧗ 1'-2'

'The tea of the Samurai'. Invigorating without inducing nervousness, This is the ideal tea to accompany mental and physical exertion. Its taste is vigorous, delicate and fresh.
Tasting recommendations: 0,2 oz of tea in 180ml of water at 140°F for one and a half minute.

REF. 301

Selection of Green teas Gift box.
12 tubes of tea – Ref. DCMVE

JAPAN

Sencha Ariake

☀ 🌡 160°F   ⧗ 1'-2'

Produced by the province of Kyushu, Sencha Ariake is the mildest of the great Sencha teas. Very invigorating and flowery, it is very pleasing in the morning. Drinking recommendations: 0,35 oz of tea in 450ml of water at 160°F for 1 to 2 minutes.

LOOSE: REF. 302

IN A TIN (100G): REF. DVN302

IN MUSLIN BAGS: REF. D302S

Sencha Supérieur

☀ 🌡 170°F   ⧗ 2'-3'

This Sencha tea is by far the most popular in Japan. Powerful and vigorous, it is a very pleasant accompaniment to a meal. Drinking recommendations: 0,35 oz of tea in 450ml of water at 170°F for 2 to 3 minutes.

LOOSE: REF. 303

IN MUSLIN BAGS: REF. D303S

Fleur de Geisha

☀ 🌡 170°F   ⧗ 3'

Created in homage to the women of Kyoto and inspired by the Japanese tradition of *Hanami* — the contemplation of cherry blossom in the springtime — *Fleur de Geisha* tea is a refined blend of Japanese green tea, subtly scented with cherry blossom.

LOOSE: REF. 309

IN A TIN (100G): REF. DVN309

IN MUSLIN BAGS: REF. D309S

IN A WASHI CANISTER: REF. D309G

TAMARYOKUCHA

Tamaryokucha teas are produced in the same way as Sencha teas. They are simply rolled instead of being folded, which gives them more colour.

Tamaryokucha Impérial

☀ 🌡 160°F   ⧗ 2'

A remarkable green tea, the leaves of which are of a very beautiful dark green colour; a sign of high quality in this type of tea. Plucked in spring, this tea is milder than most Japanese green teas.

REF. 299

BANCHA

Bancha teas are produced with lower, larger leaves than those used for Sencha teas. The folding of the leaves is also less refined. They make up the bulk of Japanese production and are taken in three different guises: natural, grilled or with cereal grains added.

BANCHA

☀ 🌡 195°F   ⏳ 3'

A tea with a fresh and delicate taste.

REF. 307

BANCHA HOJICHA

☾ 🌡 195°F   ⏳ 3'

Bancha teas can also be grilled. It is a simple operation and Japanese teashops often roast their tea themselves. On grilling the Bancha tea takes on a brown colour and a very pleasing woody aroma. It is excellent with meals, especially with fish. It is a very thirst quenching tea, ideal in the evening.

REF. 306

GENMAICHA

☀ 🌡 180°F   ⏳ 2'-3'

Still little known outside Japan, this is an amazing mix of Bancha tea and roasted rice. Also very thirst quenching, it is a pleasant accompaniment to a savoury meal.

Worth noting: Genmaicha is equally delicious either hot or cold.

REF. 305

4 oz tea canister of Fleur de Geisha: Ref. DV309B Empty caddy: Ref. V401B

I n Japan, tea has a very important cultural dimension. More than just an art of good living, it is a cult founded on the adoration of Beauty amidst the banalities of everyday existence. This philosophy has translated itself into the form of an extremely circumscribed ceremony, which takes place in a specific place and every gesture must be strictly followed.

A maximum of five people perform the ceremony, which is held in a pavilion including a tea room and a preparation room, usually located in a specific shady part of the garden. Smaller than traditional tearooms this pavilion should give the impression of genteel poverty since asceticism conveys for the Japanese people the essence of true beauty.

This philosophical ceremony, developed towards the end of the 15th century under the influence of Zen Buddhism, invites man to purify himself by uniting with nature. This is why the walkway leading to the pavilion is lined with trees and flowers, allowing the visitor to reach the first stage of meditation. Nothing else, moreover, is left to chance: decor, food, conversational subjects, etc. Great respect is given to the *geishas* who are perfectly in control of even the smallest detail of the ceremony.

Firstly, a light meal is served,

followed by a short pause. Then comes the *Goza Iri*, the central moment of the ceremony during which first a thick tea is served – *Koicha* – then a light one – *Usucha*. Various cleansing rituals and courtesies take place until the host hits a gong five times. After a series of meticulous gestures, he pours into a bowl three spoonfuls of Matcha per guest, adds a ladleful of hot water and beats it with a bamboo whisk until a thick liquid has been produced. The bowl is placed next to the hearth and the guest of honour approaches on his knees. He then takes three sips and, after the first one offers his compliments on the taste of the tea. He then dries the place where his lips touched the bowl, with the *Kaishi* paper that he brought with him, and passes the bowl to the second guest who proceeds in the same way and so forth. The last person gives the bowl back to the first guest, who hands it over to the host.

The different stages of the Cha No Yu ceremony have been of the utmost importance in the development of Japanese architecture, gardening,

TAKE PART IN THE JAPANESE TEA CEREMONY WITH THE TEA SCHOOL

GO FURTHER WITH
L'ÉCOLE
DU THÉ

landscaping, its china and floral art. Each step involves aesthetic awareness and compliance in different areas. For example, it's valuing the tools necessary for the ceremony: the bowl, the box, the ladle, the whisk; these are often true works of art. But it is also about knowing how to relish their decorative settings, such as the *Kakemono*, a vertical painting on a roller, the *Chabana*, a flower arrangement designed for the occasion or even the harmony played out by the slopes of the teahouse roofs.

Furthermore, the meticulous etiquette during this ceremony has deeply influenced the conduct and social graces of Japanese people. To understand that this ancient art, is designed to give grace and good manners to those who practise it, is one of the keys to understanding Japanese society.

The cast iron Japanese teapots come from the region of Iwate, to the north east of Honshu. They are handmade, using ancient techniques that date back to the 12th century.

During this period, at the instigation of Nambu Toshinao, feudal lord of the district of Nambu (Iwate's old name), craftsmen began to mine the region's iron ore and create cast iron artefacts, for the preparation of tea. News of their skill soon travelled beyond the borders of Nambu and orders began to flood in from all over Japan. Since then, the success of cast iron kettles and braziers from Nambu has never faltered.

Throughout the centuries, many artists have expressed themselves in the creation of cast iron artefacts, and in doing so have built up an extraordinary heritage, providing countless sources of inspiration. Today, some of the ancient designs are still manufactured alongside the most recent creations of the great Japanese designers.

The appearance of cast iron teapots is more recent and is, in fact, the result of a misuse that Westerners made of the traditional kettles.

How to take care of your teapot?

If you wish to take good care of a cast iron teapot and preserve its qualities and beauty, please follow these instructions.

● after having used the teapot, rinse it out with hot water. Under no circumstances use detergents,
● dry the outside surfaces while they are still warm,

Taira-Nami Teapot 0.55 l
Pastel blue
Ref. M198A

Taira-Nami Teapot 0.55 l
Sky blue
Ref. M198B

Taira-Nami Teapot 0.55 l
Aozumi blue
Ref. M198C

- never scour the teapot with an abrasive object (a 'Scotch Brite' sponge etc), but wipe with a soft cloth,
- always allow the inside of the teapot to air dry without the lid on,
- never leave water or tea in the teapot for too long,
- in order to avoid stains and rings, never leave water or tea on the outside surfaces of the teapot,
- before putting the teapot away, ensure that it is completely dry (inside and out) and, if possible, store it separately from its lid.

Cast iron, before it is treated, is a grey metal. Its surface can be coloured, using different processes with pigments of a wide range of colours. With the passing of time these pigments can fade slightly and give the teapot an attractive burnished hue. To avoid the spread of this natural patina, it is best to keep the teapot away from all detergents, greasy substances, dampness or direct sources of heat.

Cast iron, as its name suggests, is an iron-based alloy. Traditionally, the Japanese have allowed their teapots to rust, which is completely harmless to their health and, in fact, provides a extra source of iron to their diet. However, most teapots exported to the West have a special coating to prevent this kind of oxidation. The inside surfaces are therefore protected with a food-safe lacquer, which stops them from being porous and becoming seasoned.

India is the biggest tea producer as it accounts for almost one third of world production.

There are great differences from one type of Indian tea to another. On the one hand, this is due to the climat and local conditions which can vary greatly from one region to another: from mountainous regions to plateaux or plains; on the other hand because the plantations are not all made up of the same type of tea plant: *camelia assamica* in Assam, *camelia sinensis* in the south of India, both varieties in Darjeeling, hybridising etc.

▨ DARJEELING

Darjeelings are high altitude teas, cultivated on plantations between 0,25 and 1,5 mi above sea level, in the foothills of the Himalayas, on the outskirts of the town Darjeeling, famed for its cool and pure climate. The English started the first plantation in 1856: Tukvar, later to become Puttabong and North Tukvar. The quality of the teas and their success encouraged the rapid start up of other plantations: Dooteriah in 1859, Ging, Ambootiah, Tukdah, Phoobsering between 1860 and 1864, Badamtam, Makaibari later.

The growth of Darjeeling was extremely fast and there are still 90 plantations today. For a long time, 61 of these have been classified into three categories, according to their altitude. If, at one time, these categories may have had some meaning in terms of prestige and

fame, today they no longer make sense, since the quality of the crop on all the plantations has improved, and depends as much on the skill of the planter as on the plantation's altitude.

Darjeeling, because of its high price, is a tea that is reserved for export. It is sold in two ways:

● as a 'blend': a mixture from different plantations, all designated with the generic name of 'Darjeeling'.
● in the original tea chests, in the case of the rarest and finest teas, which carry the relevant information: the name of the plantation, the grade and the time of plucking.

Darjeeling is one of the most prestigious teas in the world. Its flavour and scent can be very different from one crop to another and from one plantation to another. This depends on:
● the time of plucking (spring, summer, autumn, during the monsoon),
● the way in which the tea is plucked,
● the climatic conditions,
● the altitude and the direction the plantation faces in relation to the sun,
● the distribution of tea plants on the plantation: whether they come from Assam, China, are cloned etc.
● the soil on the plantation, rather like the grape variety for wine.

first flush

The spring flush of Darjeeling, the first of five harvests, usually takes place between the end of February and the end of April. It is an event keenly anticipated by the world's tea lovers, since spring Darjeelings, which are produced in very limited quantities, are rare teas, with great aromatic richness, the fineness of which has earned them the nickname of the 'Champagne of teas'.

First flush
Singbulli

Throughout the whole winter, the tea plant is allowed to rest and its shoots become full of essential oils. The very first harvests of the year contain a very high percentage of these young shoots, known as 'golden tips' and are often of a very high grade. A spring Darjeeling can be easily recognized by the green hue the leaf takes on when it is infused. Young and light, its bouquet is fresh and lively.

Second flush
Puttabong Muscatel

An essential factor for the first flush is the climatic conditions that precede it; the quality and the flavour of the teas are closely dependent on them and the same plantation can produce very different teas from one year to the next. Every year therefore, Le Palais des Thés experts go to Darjeeling to taste the product of each plantation so they can make their selection from amongst the best teas and then send them to France.

Third flush
Badamtam

INDIA

This selection is often available from March onwards for airfreighted teas and from May-June for those shipped by sea.

The fineness and freshness of spring Darjeelings make them very fragile teas that do not age well. To enjoy them at the peak of their quality, it is therefore recommended to drink them 'new season', in other words during the nine to twelve months following the harvest. To fully appreciate their richness infuse them in gentle simmering spring water for 2 to 3 minutes.

Look for the list of spring Darjeelings in the price list for the current year.

■ in-between flush

This is a fairly rare harvest, carried out in early May on some plantations, which combines the freshness of the first flush with the roundness of the summer ones.

GIELLE F.T.G.F.O.P.

◆ ♨ 205°F   ⏳ 3'-4'

A very attractive tea, typical of the intermediate crops produced each year in India.

PHOTO P. 15.

REF. 017

■ second flush

This harvest is plucked between May and June, during the hot season before the monsoon. The leaf is darker than the spring crops; it has a brown colour and is small. When infused it is shiny and copper-coloured, with a powerful bouquet.

The liqueur, round and golden, is more full-bodied than it is for the first flush. Very aromatic and relatively astringent at the same time, it is long-lasting in the mouth and often has a taste of ripe fruit. These teas can be infused for 3 to 5 minutes, according to taste and depending on the number of leaves being infused. For a more scented tea, it is possible to increase the quantity of leaves together with the amount of water, while decreasing the length of infusion.

We source our permanent selection of teas from estates with well-established reputations, having established a working relationship with growers over many years' collaboration.

The price list for the current year also includes a selection of Rare and Ephemeral Second Flush darjeelings. Harvested in very small quantities and available while stocks last, these teas are not intended for inclusion in the permanent catalogue range.

PUTTABONG F.T.G.F.O.P.

♣ 🌡 205°F   ⏳ 3'-5'

One of the most prestigious tea garden, the oldest in Darjeeling, which is famed for its bud-rich harvests. The second flush produces a dark infusion and a deep and amber-coloured liqueur with lots of body. Its taste, full-bodied and woody, makes it an ideal morning tea.

REF. 021

CASTLETON F.T.G.F.O.P.

♣ 🌡 205°F   ⏳ 3'-5'

One of the most highly regarded gardens in Darjeeling, the product of which is very consistent. Fine and robust, this tea develops complex aromatic notes in the cup: flowery and woody at the same time. The two characteristics are balanced well.

REF. 022

MARGARET'S HOPE F.T.G.F.O.P.

♣ 🌡 205°F   ⏳ 3'-5'

Fruity with a great character. Special feature: it is invigorating and dark because of the greater proportion of Assam tea plants (20%) on the plantation, something that is not very common in Darjeeling. It is a much sought after tea, which Darjeeling enthusiasts find ideal in the morning.

LOOSE: REF. 018

IN A TIN (100G): DVN018

IN MUSLIN TEAS BAGS: REF. D018S

DJ, BATCH NUMBER

First flush Darjeelings are not only identified by a grade and the estate name, but also by a batch number (consisting of the letters 'DJ' followed by a number). Hence, 'Singbulli DJ 7' indicates the seventh batch of the year, harvested and processed in the Singbulli plantation. Even batches sourced in a single garden offer distinct organoleptic characteristics, resulting from the quality of the plucking as well as the weather conditions on the day that the tea is harvested and processed.

DARJEELING THURBO F.T.G.F.O.P.
♠ ♨ 205°F   ⧖ 3'-5'

A carefully selected harvest with a high bud content. A very good afternoon tea with well developed flowery aromas.
REF. 020

HIGH BLEND G.F.O.P.
♠ ♨ 205°F   ⧖ 3'-5'
A blend from the great plantations. Produces an amber-coloured, sweet and flowery infusion.
REF. 027

▥ monsoon flush

Tea produced during the monsoon season, from July to September, is of a lower quality than the other harvests. In fact, it is lacking sun.

▥ third flush

This harvest gives a tea with large leaves. The liqueur is darker than the second harvest and its aroma more powerful.

OAKS F.T.G.F.O.P.
♠ ♨ 205°F   ⧖ 3'-5'
To be drunk throughout the day. An autumn plucking with a powerful aroma.
PHOTO P. 73
REF. 030

■ Darjeeling blends

GRAND HIMALAYA F.T.G.F.O.P.
🍃 🌡 205°F   ⏳ 3'30"-4'
A blend from the three flushes.
REF. 015

■ semi fermented Darjeeling

Semi fermented teas are a speciality of Taiwan and the Fujian region in China. It is rarely produced by other countries.

DARJEELING WU LONG
☾ 🌡 205°F   ⏳ 5'-7'
Two successful personalities together: the woody Wu Long (oolong) teas and the more vigorous, aromatic Darjeeling teas. Highly sought after by enthusiasts of fine teas, this Darjeeling is ideal for the evening.
REF. 045

■ green Darjeeling

Though traditional in China and Japan, unfermented tea is still a rarity in the north of India.

THÉ DES SHERPAS T.G.F.O.P.
☀ 🌡 180°F   ⏳ 3'
A green tea with many buds. Fresh and scented, its taste brings to mind roasted chestnuts.
REF. 046

THÉ DES MOINES

Inspired by an ancient recipe developed in a Tibetan monastery Thé des Moines is a rare blend with a unique flavour.

Tibetan legend has it that a community of monks used to prepare a blend of tea, plants and flowers in the utmost secrecy. After a few days of soaking, the leaves were carefully plucked out and put to one side. By this mysterious alchemy the monks turned the tea into gold and gave Thé des Moines its exceptional scent.

The precious tea was then stored in little clay pots sealed by the rope belt from a monk's habit. In this way Thé des Moines could be preserved for many months still retaining its bewitching scent.

Brown, sand-coloured or black pot of Thé des Moines
Ref. D898P (B, J or N)

■ ASSAM

The province of Assam is situated in the northeast of India, to the east of Darjeeling between Bangladesh, Myanmar (Burma) and China. It is a low-lying region, criss-crossed by the Brahmapoutre and its tributaries, that was covered, in the early 20th century, with tropical rainforest. This fertile region produces more than half of India's tea. The rainfall is the same as in Darjeeling (dry from November to January and wet from April to September) but the rain is much heavier. Two harvests are possible: the first flush however takes place very rarely, the bulk of the output comes between April and October. Assam teas are vigorous, spicy, tannic and astringent, typically known as 'British taste'. The infusion is generous and very dark; the liqueur is dark and powerful, and can sometimes be drunk with milk.

These teas are found in all the full-bodied morning blends (see Traditional English blends on page 102). If not blended, they must be sold under their label of origin, in other words under the name of the plantation that produced them.

■ second flush, whole leaves

MAIJIAN T.G.F.O.P.

■ ♨ 205°F   ⌛ 3'-4'

One of the best Assams. This tea is worth noting due to the size of its leaves and the number of its golden buds. It gives an amber-coloured liqueur with a sustained scent. Of very great fineness, the taste is flowery and long lasting in the mouth.
REF. 052

HATTIALI T.G.F.O.P.

■ ♨ 205°F   ⌛ 3'-4'

A very good Assam with a large leaf and a high bud count. It has a pronounced and very spicy aroma. The liqueur is dark and full-bodied, which makes it a very high quality Assam that is perfect in the morning.
REF. 053

BHOOTEACHANG T.G.F.O.P.

🍃 🌡 205°F   ⏳ 3'-4'

Lots of golden tips. A lightly full-bodied and balanced tea, whose delicate, nutmeg aroma is fairly unusual for an Assam.

REF. 055

BAZALONI T.G.F.O.P.

🍃 🌡 205°F   ⏳ 3'-4'

The strongest of the whole leaf Assams. Its peppery taste makes it the 'English' tea par excellence.

REF. 054

JAIPUR T.G.F.O.P.

🍃 🌡 205°F   ⏳ 3'-4'

Rich in buds, mild and aromatic at the same time and slightly astringent.

REF. 056

▩ second flush, broken leaves

HAJUA F.T.G.B.O.P.

🍃 🌡 205°F   ⏳ 2'-4'

This is the tea with the highest bud count of the broken leaf Assams.

REF. 062

ORGANIC TEAS

Le Palais des Thés offers a selection of famous label teas that have been grown organically. These can change from year to year. You will find them in the price list for the year in progress.

MIJICAJAN G.B.O.P.

🍃 🌡 205°F   ⏳ 2'-4'

A strong, aromatic, 'English style' tea.

REF. 064

▩ SIKKIM

This small Himalayan state produces a fine and aromatic tea that is a close cousin of the best Darjeelings, to which it is also geographically close.

TEMI T.G.F.O.P.

🍃 🌡 205°F   ⏳ 3'-5'

An outstanding garden. As flowery but less powerful than a summer Darjeeling. Highly recommended. Best very early in the morning.

REF. 080

India, Nepal and Sri Lanka Gift box.
12 tubes of tea from these three countries - Ref. DCMIE

A WORD FROM AN EXPERT:
ANIL DHARMAPALAN
Manager of the Thiashola plantation

'I have been manager of Thiashola for many years. My plantation mainly produces broken teas for the local market. However we have a tradition, here at Thiashola, of offering a whole leaf tea to guests who stay at the plantation.

I met Le Palais des Thés team in 1999 while they were on a sourcing trip in the Nilgiri Mountains. Thiashola was one of the stopping points on their journey. I think that Francois-Xavier Delmas must have been truly seduced by our whole leaf. He very quickly asked to buy it in considerable quantities so that he could introduce it to his customers. Since then, we have kept a larger area of tea plants to the growing of Thiashola's 'Carrington' and we are always delighted to produce this visitors' tea for our friends at the Le Palais des Thés.'

▩ NILGIRI

Nilgiri, which is situated in the south of India, is the second biggest tea-producing region after Assam. This region of plateaux of the same height as those in Sri Lanka, produces teas whose regular leaf and round, full bodied liqueur recall Sri Lankan teas.

THIASHOLA 'CARRINGTON'
S.F.T.G.F.O.P.1

🍃 🌡 205°F ⏳ 4'-5'

A superb leaf which gives a round and mellow tea; fruity and aromatic and a worthy representative of the best high altitude teas of the subcontinent. An exceptional crop, reserved for visitors to the plantation, of which Le Palais des Thés has managed to secure a few chests.

LOOSE: REF. 195

4 oz tea canister of Thé des Moines: Ref. DV898C Empty caddy: V401C

THIASHOLA F.B.O.P.
◆ ♨ 205°F   ⧖ 3'-5'

One of the best broken black teas.
REF. 196

TIGER HILL O.P.
◆ ♨ 205°F   ⧖ 4'-5'
Round and full-bodied.
REF. 191

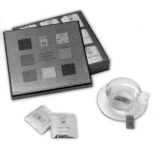

Fine Teas Selection Box.
The box-set contains 54 muslin tea bags,
i.e. 6 of 9 different varieties
of the finest single-origin teas.
Each tea bag contains around 0,1 oz of tea.
See box-set P. 103, 118.

THÉ DES FAKIRS

In India the introduction of tea by the English and the discovery of wild tea plants in Assam dates back to the early 19th century. At first produced for the British market, tea has gradually become a very popular drink throughout Indian society. While certain castes still prepare it in a typically English way, the tea that is taken daily by the vast majority of Indians is a surprising mixture of black tea, spices and sugar, infused into boiling whole milk: Chai, pronounced 'Tchai'.

Inspired by the Chai tradition, Thé des Fakirs is a tasty, scented blend of green tea, cardamom and cloves with a hint of grapefruit.

Thé des Fakirs in a tea canister
Ref. D875F

SRI LANKA

In 1972 the island of Ceylon changed its name to Sri Lanka, but its former name, which dates back to the British Empire, has remained in use within the world of tea. It is not unusual to speak of a 'Ceylon' to describe a tea from this country. Sri Lanka, nicknamed the tea island, is the third largest producer in the world and supplies more than half of the black tea consumed in France.

The English introduced the tea plant in 1857 but it was not really developed until after 1870: in essence tea cultivation in Sri lanka owes its development to the total destruction, in 1869, by a parasite of the coffee plantations which used to cover the entire island.

Sri Lankan teas come from six regions located in the south of the island at altitudes ranging from sea level up to 1,55 mi. Plucking seasons vary from region to region, depending on when the monsoon is expected that year. A Sri Lankan tea can be recognized by its superb copper colour and its lively, piquant scent. As for the taste, this varies from one region to another, with the higher altitude teas very often being the best.

As in India, tea growing is organized into gardens, with the name being specified whenever a tea comes exclusively from one of them and has not been blended with any other teas.

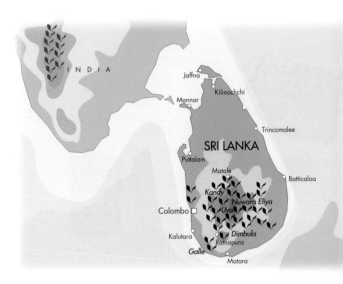

THE NUWARA ELIYA DISTRICT

A high altitude region that is hardly touched by the monsoon. Plucking takes place between February and April for the best quality. Teas from this region can be recognised by a bronze colour the leaves take on when they are infused. The liqueur is very clear and amber-coloured and its taste is flowery and evokes jasmine.

SAM BODHI F.O.P.

☀ 🌡 205°F   ⧖ 3'-5'

One of the most handsome teas of this district. Very rich in buds, its infusion is dark and produces a round and very flowery liqueur.

REF. 101

THE UVA DISTRICT

A region of intermediate altitude, notable for its season of dry winds (June to September), which give the Uva region teas their main characteristics: a copper-coloured infusion, mellow and aromatic teas with a round taste, but less full-bodied than other Sri Lankan teas.

NELUWA O.P.

◆ 🌡 205°F   ⧖ 4'-5'

One of the best high altitude tea in Sri Lanka. Both dark and aromatic. The liqueur is velvety.

REF. 104

SAINT-JAMES O.P.

☀ 🌡 205°F   ⧖ 4'-5'

A prestigious grand old garden, whose reputation has travelled around the globe. A light and copper-coloured infusion, with an almost chocolaty taste.

This tea is also available in muslin bags.

LOOSE: REF. 111

IN A TIN (100G): REF. DVN111

IN MUSLIN BAGS: REF. D111S

SAINT-JAMES B.O.P.

☀ 🌡 205°F   ⧖ 3'-5'

An outstanding broken tea from the plantation mentioned above. Astringent and fruity, it can take the addition of a dash of milk.

REF. 121

SAINT-JAMES FANNINGS F.

◆ 🌡 205°F   ⧖ 2'-5'

A crushed tea, good for breakfast with milk.

REF. 180

DISTRICT DE RATNAPURA

NEW VITHANAKANDE F.B.O.P.F.E.X.S

☀ 🌡 195°F   ⧖ 4'

The best of the low-grown Sri Lankan teas. Though this tea represents just 1% of the production of this garden, in the space of a few years it has become sought-after by connoisseurs for its great subtlety and rich aromas.

RÉF. 115

■ THE DIMBULA DISTRICT

The district around Dimbula is drenched by the monsoon rains from June to September. Plucking takes place from January to mid March. The teas are full-bodied and astringent. They produce a light brown infusion and a dark liqueur.

PETTIAGALLA O.P.
☀ 🌡 205°F   ⏳ 4'-5'
A great high altitude tea. A superb, very regular leaf. One of the best Orange Pekoe in the district with a full-bodied, rich aroma.
REF. 114

■ THE KANDY DISTRICT

This low-lying district produces good quality teas that are full-bodied and astringent.

KALLEBOCKA F.O.P.
☀ 🌡 205°F   ⏳ 4'-5'
A powerful, malty afternoon tea.
REF. 102

■ THE GALLE DISTRICT

This district, located in the south of the island, is renowned for its Orange Pekoe with their highly worked and very regular leaves. Their aroma is powerful and long lasting in the mouth.

GALABODA O.P.
☀ 🌡 205°F   ⏳ 4'-5'
Full-bodied and slightly astringent, this is an excellent Orange Pekoe for the morning.
REF. 106

■ BLENDS

CEYLAN STRONG BREAKFAST
🌓 🌡 205°F   ⏳ 3'-5'
A very full-bodied breakfast tea.
REF. 190

Nepal, Sikkim and Bangladesh

Nepal

Nepal, an independent Himalayan kingdom, produces a tea that is a cousin of Darjeeling tea in its appearance, aroma and its ripe fruit taste. For the past two decades, small-scale plantations in the east of the country have been producing some of the best teas in the world. Find a selection of the finest Nepalese teas in this year's price list.

Ilam t.g.f.o.p.

🔔 🌡 205°F   ⏳ 3'-5'

A very good tea, flowery and slightly astringent. Darker than a summer Darjeeling.

REF. 090

Bangladesh

Close to Assam, Bangladesh tea grows in the north of the country, near the border with India. Highly coloured and aromatic, it can be taken with a little milk.

Bangladesh t.g.f.o.p.

🔔 🌡 205°F   ⏳ 4'-5'

A handsome whole leaf suitable for daytime drinking. Mild and amber-coloured.

REF. 095

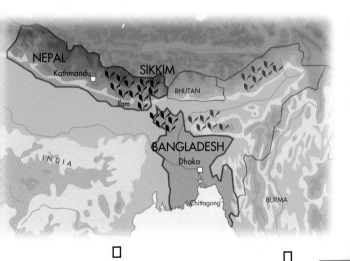

Tea arrived in this region via different routes and was at first a commodity imported from far away, long before it began to be grown at home. It was the Mongols and the merchants of the Silk Route that introduced tea to the Russians, the Turks, the Persians as well as the peoples of Kirghistan, Turkmenistan, Uzbekistan... Towards the end of the 19th century and the beginning of the 20th, the numerous attempts to grow tea plants in the area became successful in the mountains between the Caspian Sea and the Black Sea. Iran, Turkey and the CIS, who specialize in the preparation of black tea in a samovar, produce tea mainly for their own consumption. The former USSR was, at one time, the fifth largest producer in the world. We must be careful not to confuse teas from this country, sometimes categorized as 'Russian style' teas because of their use in the samovar, with the 'Russian taste' label given to some blends of Chinese black teas, scented or not, which were made popular by the Russian court at the end of the 19th century.

(See page 109).

Turkey

As in many countries in this region, the drinking of tea pre-dates its cultivation, and it was in the 16th century that the beverage was introduced to the Ottoman court. As far as cultivation was concerned, it started in the 1920s, using seeds from the Soviet Union. The plantations cover the south shores of the Black Sea between Rize and Trabzon and are often small in size where a more collective style of farming is practised. Turkey is the sixth largest tea producer in the world and its output is self-sufficient with small-scale export. Turkish style tea, prepared in a samovar, is most commonly served with nothing added, but can also have the addition of pine nuts or cardamom seeds. It is a delicious accompaniment to Turkish delight, gazelle's horn and other eastern pastries.

Bas-Caucase b.o.p.

☀ ꙮ 205°F   ⌛ 3'-5'

A scented, aromatic afternoon tea. A good samovar tea.

LOOSE: REF. 410

IN A TIN (100G): REF. DVN410

Georgia

One of the few countries, along with Japan, to have mechanized tea plucking, Georgia is one of the smaller tea producing nations. The tea plants, grown along the banks of the Black Sea, were chosen for their hardiness and are particularly resistant to cold: the Georgian plantations are some of the most northerly on the planet and winters there are harsher than on any other plantations. While this country's teas cannot be compared to the great classic teas, there are nonetheless some good black teas for drinking throughout the day.

Georgia o.p.

☀ ꙮ 205°F   ⌛ 4'-5'

A handsome whole leaf. A good samovar tea.

REF. 400

IRAN

Tea drinking in Iran dates back to the end of the 15th century. It owes its development to the difficulty of importing coffee, which was greatly enjoyed at the time but very hard to obtain from the producing countries. Taking the same route as the Silk Route, tea gradually began to replace coffee in the preferences and customs of the Mongols.

It was not until the end of the 19th century that the first attempt was made to cultivate the tea plant and not until the beginning of the 20th that the first crop of Iranian tea was sold on the local market. Plantations then developed rapidly in the province of Gilan, located between the south shore of the Caspian Sea and the Elbourz Mountains. From 1920 onwards, production underwent a real boom. Today Iran is the eighth largest producer in the world and consumes almost its entire output of tea.

GILAN O.P.

☀ ♨ 205°F   ⏳ 4'-5'

A robust and good samovar tea.

REF. 420

THÉ DU HAMMAM

A symbol of relaxation and self-abandonment, the Hammam is a place to forget everything, dedicated to the body and its well-being. In this closed and reassuring world, the art of taking one's time and taking care of oneself is rediscovered.

Thé du Hammam is inspired by a traditional Turkish recipe, based on green tea, flowers and fruit. Enlivened, in the purest of eastern traditions, with rose petals and orange flower water, Thé du Hammam is a green tea perfumed with the flesh of green dates and red fruit. This green tea, is famous for its freshness and for its thirst quenching qualities.

4 oz tea canister of Thé du Hammam:
Ref. DV861D
Empty caddy: Ref. V401D

See Thé du Hammam P.114

The first evidence of tea in Russia dates back to 1567: two Cossacks – Petrov and Yalychev – referred to it as a wonderful Chinese beverage and decided to drink it regularly. However, it was not until the end of the 17th century that tea became a staple commodity, being imported regularly into Moscow. For nearly two centuries, tea was only available in this city and remained the sole preserve of Muscovites, who were called in a mocking way by other Russians 'tea drinkers' or 'hot water drinkers'. It was only from the 1850s onwards that tea drinking spread throughout the empire and was taken up by all

social classes.

Tea in Russia is inseparable from the samovar. Invented at the beginning of the 18th century in the Urals, this artefact essential for preparing tea was widely adopted at the same time as tea became more accessible. The samovar is a kind of large kettle for making tea which contains several litres of water kept at the right temperature and is also a source of heat around which the whole family keeps warm.

The samovar is made up of a hearth, a large container with its centre hollowed out and a chimney. A wood burning stove is lit in the hearth, which serves

THE SAMOVAR

to heat the air in the chimney above it: this system allows the water to be brought to and to be kept at a constant temperature. The shape of the samovar is designed so that one can hear the various stages in the boiling of the water: it starts by 'singing' then 'humming' and finally by 'rumbling like thunder'. When the water hums, it is ready.

A tap, situated on the outer wall, allows cups and teapots to be filled easily. The teapot, in which a highly concentrated extract of tea has been prepared, is placed above the chimney and is thus kept warm. Each person serves himself/herself by pouring a little tea from the pot into a cup and then diluting it with hot water. To cool the beverage, the contents of the cup are often emptied into a saucer and the tea is drunk directly from this second receptacle.

Tea occupies a prominent place in Russian society and has even given the language some of its

EXPLORE RUSSIAN TRADITIONS WITH THE TEA SCHOOL

Go further with L'ÉCOLE DU THÉ

common idiomatic expressions: a 'tip' for example is a 'na tchaï' which means 'for the tea'. On a social level, getting together for a cup of tea had different functions: starting as an intimate family gathering, it became a social event in which the high society and formal side of things completely masked any warmth and cosiness.

Today, drinking a cup of tea around the samovar means performing a warm and friendly action, similar in function to the original family gatherings, of which one can find descriptions in all 19th and early 20th centuries Russian literature. It is a time of sharing with family and friends, when everyone stops for a minute to feel the warmth and enjoy everyone else's presence.

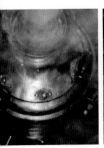

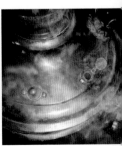

The introduction of tea to Africa goes back to the end of the 19th century. It first originated in South Africa where the English started its cultivation to secure new sources of supply. Then, German settlers experimented with its cultivation on the slopes of Mount Cameroon and in Tanzania. Throughout the 20th century numerous countries began to grow tea, and today, the African continent is an important player in the world tea market.

The teas are produced either by using traditional methods, giving either broken or whole leaf teas (see pages 18-19), or equally they are produced by CTC, 'crushing, tearing, curling', a mechanical process that transforms the tea leaf into tiny pearls mainly for teabags. Today a dozen African countries produce black tea, of an uneven quality depending on its origin, and Le Palais des Thés experts have decided to only buy the product from some of them.

AFRICA

■ KENYA

Kenya is the fourth largest producer in the world today, contributing to 8% of the total production. Almost all the teas from the country are CTC teas with the exception of the Marynin garden which has kept its traditional processing methods.

MARYNIN F.O.P.
🔔 🌡 205°F   ⏳4'-5'
Close to an Assam, with which it shares the nutmeg taste. Its low astringency makes it a very pleasant afternoon tea.
REF. 501

MARYNIN BROKEN F.B.O.P.
🔔 🌡 205°F   ⏳3'-5'
A superb broken leaf tea, aromatic and full-bodied.
REF. 505

■ RWANDA

Rwanda's tea production is completely minor on a world scale but the country offers certain teas of a very interesting quality.

■ ZIMBABWE

MUKUMBANI FANNINGS F.
🔔 🌡 205°F   ⏳2'-5'
This will suit the enthusiasts of very full-bodied morning teas. Best drank with milk.
REF. 525

■ CAMEROON

CAMEROON B.O.P.
🔔 🌡 205°F   ⏳3'-5'
A pleasant, fairly full-bodied, morning tea that takes the addition of milk well. If used in a blend, it brings more body.
REF. 530

■ MAURITIUS

Mauritius, which is close to Reunion, produces various teas, the most famous of them is appreciated for its vanilla taste.

MAURITIUS
☀ 🌡 205°F   ⏳4'-5'

An excellent black tea, evoking vanilla, citrus and red fruit.
LOOSE: REF. 350
IN A TIN (100G): REF. DVN350

◼ ROOIBOS

Native from South Africa, the *Aspalathus linearis*, or *Rooibos bush* as it is commonly known, is a different plant from the tea plant, which gives a pleasant beverage with no caffeine and almost no tannin.

ROOIBOS
☾ ♨ 205°F　　　　⧖5'
REF. 910

MÉLANGE DU CAP
☾ ♨ 205°F　　　　⧖5'
'Cape Blend'. With splinters of cocoa bean and vanilla pods.
REF. 915

WINDHUK
☾ ♨ 205°F　　　　⧖5'
A delicate vanilla scent.
REF. 917

PRETORIA
☾ ♨ 205°F　　　　⧖5'
Scented with wild cherry.
REF. 918

THÉ DES SABLES

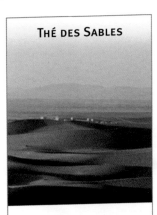

With Thé des Sables, Le Palais des Thés would like to introduce you to the rose of Damascus, a rose that grows on the slopes of mount Atlas, in the south of Morocco. It is named after the Syrian capital from where it was brought, some hundreds of years ago, as part of the merchandise of a caravan train. Its scent is powerful and sensual, almost peppery. It is used whole as a spice in certain North African dishes, but it is especially in the form of a petals preserve that it conveys all its flavour. Combined with hot weather fruit — citrus fruit, mangoes and yellow peaches — and with the freshness of green tea, the rose of Damascus gives to Thé des Sables its incomparable scent of preserved rose.

Thé des Sables - Ref. 858

4 oz tea canister of Thé des Vahinés "Rooibos".
Réf. DV856F
Empty caddy:
Ref. V401F

In a 9th century commercial report the Arab merchant Suleiman told of his travels in China. He mentioned tea as an almost sacred herb, the importance of which was essential in Chinese society; outside Chinese texts, this is the oldest written record about the existence of tea. Tea arrived in Egypt towards the 16th century, having passed through Pakistan, the Arabian Peninsula and Turkey. But its progress stopped there and it did not get past the Libyan Desert.

In fact, it was not until the middle of the 19th century that tea is introduced to the countries of the Maghreb, at a time when the English, faced with the loss of the Slavonic market after the Crimean war, were looking for new openings. They turned to sell their supply towards Morocco, and more specifically towards the ports of Mogador and Tangier. The most popular beverage at the time in Maghreb was an infusion of mint leaves, sometimes of absinthe. Tea was favourably received by the people since, by mixing it with these leaves, it made them less bitter without spoiling their flavour or their colour. It was rapidly adopted and the traditional Moroccan way of drinking tea was born. Thanks to nomadic people tea drinking soon spread all over the Maghreb and the whole of West Africa. Ever since, serving mint tea has become part of the rulebook for good living, not only in Morocco but also in many other Arab countries.

The tea used is always green tea, usually Gunpowder, which is known for its freshness and thirst quenching qualities.

Tea represents the most refined expression of hospitality. It is usually the head of the household who prepares it, sometimes his eldest son, unless he wishes to honour his guest by inviting him to carry out the task. Two teapots are prepared at the same time: the person officiating puts a large pinch of green tea in each one, which he then quickly rinses with boiling water to take away its bitterness. A handful of mint leaves and a large piece of sugar loaf are then added to each teapot, and covered with boiling water. After a few minutes of infusion,

TAKE PART IN THE MOROCCAN RITUAL WITH THE TEA SCHOOL

GO FURTHER WITH L'ÉCOLE DU THÉ

the person making the tea stirs the mixture and tastes it, adding a few more leaves or a little more sugar if needed. Next, he lifts both teapots up high and then pours the tea into the small glasses, which he will carry on a finely engraved metal tray. Three successive infusions are served, each one sweeter than the last, and after the final one it is polite for the guest to signal that he will leave.

In the desert the preparation of tea is slightly different and is accomplished using small enamelled metal teapots, which are placed directly on the fire and filled with tea, water and sugar. As in Morocco, three successive teas are served: Touaregs say that the first is strong, like life; the second is good, like love and the last is sweet, like death.

The teas of South America cannot pretend to compete with the great teas of India or Sri Lanka, even if they share similar characteristics. They are completely unknown to European consumers and are still to be discovered.

ARGENTINA

The eleventh producer in the world, Argentina has been growing tea for the last sixty years or so. Almost all the plantations are to be found along the border with Brazil in the Misiones region.

FLOR DE ORO F.B.O.P.
🍃 🌡 205°F   ⏳3'-5'

A fairly full-bodied tea.
LOOSE: REF. 605

4 oz tea canister of Thé des Alizés Réf. DV862G Empty caddy: Ref. V401G

MATE

Mate does not come from tea plants but from a plant native to South America, very high in caffeine. It is also called 'Jesuits' tea'.

The word "mate" comes from the quechua, "mathi", denoting a recipient, a type of gourd traditionally used to prepare and drink mate, and which is still used today.

GREEN MATE
🍃 🌡 205°F   ⏳5'

REF. 950

BLENDS AND FLAVOURS

Besides the tea producing countries, there are numerous tea drinking countries that have developed specific recipes based on tea: blends and Earl Grey in Great Britain, Russian blends in Russia, aromatic teas and scented blends in Europe…

These teas are created using black, green or semi fermented teas to which carefully selected pieces of fruit, flowers, spices, seaweed or natural extracts are sometimes added.

Some teas are bought directly in their country of origin, such as Flowers of China tea and certain teas that are flavoured according to local tradition; most are created in France by Le Palais des Thés experts whose skill and imagination have produced some amazing mixed flavours. Their talents are testified in the success of teas such as *Big Ben*, *Vice-Roi des Indes*, *Thé des Sables*, *Thé des Lords*, *Blue of London*, *Thé du Hammam*, *Thé des Amants*, *N°25* or our famous vanilla-scented green tea.

In this section you will find teas whose preparation, beyond the plucking and the management of the fermentation process, comes close to imitate the skill of a perfumer.

TRADITIONAL ENGLISH BLENDS
- Blends
- Earl Grey

SLAVONIC SPECIALITIES
- Unscented Russian blends
- Scented Russian blends

FLOWERS OF CHINA
- Jasmine tea
- Rose tea

SCENTED BLENDS
- Mainly floral
- Mainly fruity
- Mainly citrus
- Mainly spicy
- Mainly iodised

FLAVOURED TEAS

DECAFFEINATED TEAS

Blends and flavours

Traditional english blends

Ever since colonial times, the English have created tea blends, (Darjeeling, Assam, Ceylon etc), using varying proportions depending on the time of day: teas with more body in the morning and lighter ones in the afternoon.

In line with this tradition Le Palais des Thés has created blends whose balance is geared to different moments of the day,

blends

Vice-roi des Indes t.g.f.o.p.
🫖 🌡 205°F   ⏳3'-5'
A remarkable blend of Darjeeling and Yunnan teas. Refined and delicate, this tea is both fruity and powerful. Excellent for the morning and afternoon.
REF. 706

Big Ben g.f.o.p.
🫖 🌡 205°F   ⏳3'-5'
A very good blend of Yunnan and Assam. Both mild and invigorating, round and spicy, it is a successful blend of the main characteristics of both teas. Excellent for morning tea.
LOOSE: REF. 705
IN A TIN (100g): REF. DVN705
IN MUSLIN BAGS: REF. D705S

Brunch Tea g.f.o.p.
🫖 🌡 205°F   ⏳3'-5'
With the sturdiness of Assam and the delicacy of Darjeeling. Handsome whole leaves and many golden tips.
REF. 703

Queen Blend o.p.
🫖 🌡 205°F   ⏳3'-5'
Fine and delicate, good for the afternoon. A blend of Indian and Indonesian teas, chosen for 'afternoon tea'.
REF. 711

Morning Tea f.o.p.
🫖 🌡 205°F   ⏳3'-5'
A superb blend of the great Assam and Ceylon teas. Whole leaves enlivened by golden tips.
REF. 702

FIVE O'CLOCK TEA F.O.P.

🔔 🌡 205°F ⏳ 3'-5'

A hint of Assam enhances this blend of whole leaves from Darjeeling and the highlands of Ceylon. Perfect for the afternoon.

REF. 704

IRISH BLEND F.O.P.

🔔 🌡 205°F ⏳ 3'-5'

A great Darjeeling and a Ceylon from the Uva Highlands. Whole leaves enlivened with tips.

REF. 710

BREAKFAST TEA B.O.P.

🔔 🌡 205°F ⏳ 2'-5'

A full-bodied blend of broken teas from Assam, Ceylon, India and Indonesia.

REF. 700

STRONG BREAKFAST B.O.P.

🔔 🌡 205°F ⏳ 2'-5'

A very full-bodied blend of broken teas from Assam, Ceylon, Bangladesh and Indonesia, all selected for their sturdiness.

REF. 701

QUEEN BLEND FANNINGS F.

🔔 🌡 205°F ⏳ 2'-4'

An unusual strength. A blend of teas from Africa and Ceylon, powerful and aromatic.

REF. 715

MUSLIN TEA BAGS

While travelling, in the office, in a hotel – it is not always easy to find good tea. Easy to prepare, these muslin bags allow you to take your favourite teas with you wherever you wish. Each tea bag comes in an individual stay-fresh sachet, ensuring optimal conservation.

29 types of tea are available in this format in packets of 20 bags:

- *Thé des Moines.* REF. D898S
- *Thé du Hammam.* REF. D861S
- *Thé du Hammam «Rooibos».* REF. D920S
- *Thé des Vahinés «Rooibos».* REF. D856S
- *Thé des Amants.* REF. D880S
- *Fleur de Geisha.* REF. D309S
- *Thé des Fakirs.* REF. D875S
- *Thé des Lords.* REF. D802S
- *Thé des Lords «Rooibos».* REF. D921S
- *Thé des Songes.* REF. D896S
- *Green tea with vanilla.* REF. D850S
- *Rooibos tea and verbena.* REF. D911S
- *Rooibos tea and camomile.* REF. D912S
- *Rooibos tea with lime blossom and mint.* REF. D913S
- *Big Ben.* REF. D705S
- *Blue of London.* REF. D803S
- *Grand Yunnan Impérial.* REF. D220S
- *Grand Jasmin Chun Feng.* REF. D250S
- *Margaret's Hope.* REF. D018S
- *Saint-James O.P.* REF. D111S
- *Sencha Ariake.* REF. D302S
- *Long Jing.* REF. D198S
- *Pu Er Impérial.* REF. D215S
- *Thé du Tigre.* REF. D271S
- *Thé des Sources.* REF. D857S
- *Thé des Sables.* REF. D858S
- *Thé des Alizés.* REF. D862S
- *Thé Goût Russe 7 Agrumes.* REF. D494S
- *Thé du Hammam Black Leaf.* REF. D855S

Selection of muslin tea bags box set.
Ref. DMOUS, DOR, DPAR

DÉLICES DE THÉ

DÉLICES DE THÉ

Délice de Thé is made from a recipe created by Le Palais des Thés. It is prepared from a tea brew and cane sugar. Cooked in a copper pot, these preparations release all the aromas of the great Le Palais des Thés flavoured teas.

- *Thé des Moines.* REF. F500MO
- *Thé du Hammam.* REF. F500HA
- *Thé des Songes.* REF. F500MI
- *Montagne Bleue.* REF. F500MB
- *Goût Russe 7 Agrumes.* REF. F500GR
- *Rose de Chine.* REF. F500RO

FRUIT AND DÉLICES DE THÉ

The variation of Délice de Thé combines the delicate harmonious aromas of the great teas with the sweet flavours of fresh fruit.

- *Apricot with Margaret's Hope Darjeeling.* RÉF. F551
- *Pear with Wu Long (oolong) China tea.* RÉF. F552
- *Chestnut with Taiwanese smoked tea.* RÉF. F553
- *Morello cherry with Yunnan black tea.* RÉF. F554
- *Rhubarb with Japanese green tea.* RÉF. F555

▪ Earl Grey

Earl Grey has been a great English classic ever since Charles Grey, 2nd Earl of Falloden and Foreign Secretary went on to become Prime Minister in 1830. For saving the life of the Chinese Mandarin, he received in gratitude a specially scented tea flavoured with oil of Bergamot. The Earl then introduced the tea in Britain. The quality of an Earl Grey can vary according to the bergamot being used (Calabrian and Sicilian varieties are the most famous) and the quality of the tea being flavoured.

BLUE OF LONDON, A YUNNAN EARL GREY

☀ 🌡 185°F   ⧗ 4'-5'

Yunnan is one of the best black teas in the world and with a fresh and delicate bergamot from Calabria, it gives a particularly fine and well balanced blend. An exceptional Earl Grey that will delight both fans of natural and scented teas.

LOOSE: REF. 803

IN A TIN (100G): REF. DVN803

IN MUSLIN BAGS: REF. D803S

THÉ DES LORDS
☀ 🌡 205°F   ⧖ 4'-5'

A very attractive Earl Grey with a strong bergamot scent, enlivened by safflower petals. Of all the Earl Grey teas this is the one most flavoured with bergamot.

LOOSE: REF. 802

IN A TIN (100G): REF. DVN802

IN MUSLIN BAGS: REF. D802S

THÉ DES LORDS «ROOIBOS»
☾ 🌡 205°F   ⧖ 5'

The blend, with red petals, balances the powerful lemony note of our bergamot with the roundness of Rooibos.

LOOSE: REF. 921

IN A TIN (100G): REF. DVN921

IN MUSLIN BAGS: REF. D921S

EARL GREY DARJEELING
🔔 🌡 205°F   ⧖ 3'-4'

An exceptional base tea from the highlands of the Himalayas and a delicate bergamot from Sicily.

REF. 804

EARL GREY IMPÉRIAL
☀ 🌡 205°F   ⧖ 4'-5'

Enlivened by white tips, with a good bergamot aroma.

REF. 800

EARL GREY FLEURS BLEUES
☀ 🌡 205°F   ⧖ 4'-5'

An Earl Grey enlivened by blueberry flowers. Highly scented and great fineness.

REF. 808

EARL GREY WU LONG
☾ 🌡 205°F   ⧖ 7'

A handsome, generously flavoured, Wu Long.

REF. 806

EARL GREY SENCHA
☀ 🌡 170°F   ⧖ 3'

A good blend of bergamot's sour note and the freshness of green tea.

REF. 807

4 oz tea canister of Thé des Lords:
Réf. DV802E
Empty caddy:
Réf. V401E

Blends and Flavours gift box.
12 tubes of scented teas – Ref. DCMPE

In 1606 the first tea chests arrived in Amsterdam, Holland: it was the first cargo of tea to be officially registered at a Western port. The Netherlands, at this time, had control over the trade of rare commodities from the Orient, but the English who, a few years later, founded the East India Company in direct competition with the Dutch company, soon questioned their dominance. The introduction of tea in England took place in a specific way: the coffee houses were at the time very fashionable. They were spreading rapidly and were very successful. During the same period Catherine of Bragance, a Portuguese princess and wife of the young king of England, brought as a dowry Bombay and the custom of drinking tea at anytime of the day! From then on, tea became a real craze all over the country. Having been taken up by the royal court, it was just a question of time before tea won over all levels of society and quickly became a huge popular success. Today tea is a pillar of British society and the English drink it throughout the day: starting with an 'early morning tea' often taken in bed with some plain biscuits, followed by the breakfast tea that washes down the large meal of that name, then comes 'elevenses' at 11 o'clock, which will sustain them until it is time for the traditional 'afternoon tea'. Finally, a last tea is often taken in the evening just before bedtime.

'Afternoon tea' in Great Britain is a real tradition. It is a custom that was established by the seventh Duchess of Bedford in the 19th century. At the time, lunch was taken very early and supper very late so the duchess made a habit of taking tea in the afternoon between three and four o'clock together with a light meal. She began inviting her friends to join her and thus started a fashion that enjoyed immediate and considerable success.

Today, as in the 19th century, friends or family are invited around for tea. Milk, sugar and lemon are always provided in order to cater to everyone's tastes. Tea is prepared following five cardinal rules that are typically British and are most suited to the type of tea that is drunk in England:

EXPLORE
THE ENGLISH
TRADITION WITH
THE TEA SCHOOL

GO FURTHER WITH
L'ÉCOLE
DU THÉ

● warm the teapot with boiling water, in order to warm the leaves so that they can release all their flavour,
● add one teaspoon of tea per person plus one extra for the pot,
● pour simmering, never boiling, water onto the leaves,
● leave to brew for three and five minutes,
● stir once and then serve.

When 'afternoon tea' was established, it gave rise to many artefacts, utensils, cakes… The tea caddies, tea-cosies, tea balls, tea strainers, sugar bowls, milk jugs, teacups, teapots, scones, cakes, muffins, crumpets, toasts, cream puffs etc., are all creations to bring out the best in tea, both in its the serving and in its drinking; they all contribute to the cosiness of taking tea the English way.

EARL GREY SMOKY
☀ 🌡 205°F   ⏳5'

Slightly smoked with a marked bergamot scent.

REF. 805

EARL GREY FINEST
☀ 🌡 205°F   ⏳4'-5'

The least scented with bergamot.

REF. 801

■ RUSSIAN BLENDS

One should not confuse the teas produced in Georgia with the ones that have been drunk regularly in Russia since the 17th century. These latter teas, which in the beginning were blends of black Chinese teas, became more diversified at the end of the 19th century by the introduction of Indian teas at the Russian court, most notably Darjeeling. Since then it has been the custom to refer to all blends of Darjeeling and different Chinese black teas as 'Russian blends' teas, whether or not they are scented with natural citrus extracts.

■ Unscented Russian blends

Valued for their lightness, it is mainly Qimen teas that are used in these blends, sometimes with the addition of Sichuan or Darjeeling.

MICHEL STROGOFF
☀ 🌡 205°F   ⏳4'-5'

A famous blend of teas from central Asia. A subtle balance of black and green teas, producing a powerful and invigorating beverage. Perfect for breakfast.

REF. 455

THÉ RUSSE FUMÉ
☀ 🌡 205°F   ⏳4'-5'

'Smoked Russian Tea' is a lightly smoked blend of Qimen and Sichuan teas, with a hint of jasmine flowers. Mild and flowery.

REF. 452

THÉ RUSSE
☀ 🌡 205°F   ⏳4'-5'

A good afternoon tea.

REF. 450

scented Russian blends

Like its English rival, Earl Grey, the scented Russian blends is almost always fragranced with bergamot. Some blends have other citrus fruits, and sometimes spices, as well as bergamot. Scented Russian blends teas are perfect in the afternoon.

GOÛT RUSSE 7 AGRUMES
☀ 🌡 205°F   ⏳ 4'-5'

'Russian blends with 7 citrus' an outstanding blend of black teas, lemon, lime, sweet orange, bitter orange, grapefruit, bergamot and mandarin. Created by Le Palais des Thés during its first years of existence, this cocktail of 7 citrus fruits was later added to different base teas. Often copied but never equalled, this is an exclusive Le Palais des Thés recipe. It is very good in the morning and also excellent as an iced tea.

LOOSE: REF. 494

IN MUSLIN BAGS: REF. D494S

AS A DELICE DE THE: REF. F500GR

Pack of 60 XL tea filters - Ref. W610
Pack of 100 XS individual tea filters - Ref. W611

VERS LA NUIT

Le Palais des Thés proposes a selection of totally new teas, Vers la Nuit, which teams Rooibos tea of South Africa with aromatic plants, originating in France and taken from the best varieties.
Appreciated for its high polyphenol content, Rooibos tea comes from a plant that is quite distinct from the tea bush and produces a delicious drink.
An invitation to rest and relaxation, this will send you off on a restful night's sleep.

• *Rooibos tea and verbena*
LOOSE: REF. 911
IN A TIN (100G) : REF. DVN911
IN MUSLIN BAGS: REF. D911S

• *Rooibos tea and camomile*
LOOSE: REF. 912
IN A TIN (100G) : REF. DVN912
IN MUSLIN BAGS: REF. D912S

• *Rooibos tea with lime blossom and mint*
LOOSE: REF. 913
IN A TIN (100G): REF. DVN913
IN MUSLIN BAGS: REF. D913S

DARJEELING 7 AGRUMES
🍃 🌡 205°F   ⏳3'-5'

The natural extracts that make the success of Russian blends with Darjeeling 7 citrus fruits here scent an outstanding Darjeeling.

LOOSE: REF. 490

WU LONG 7 AGRUMES
☾ 🌡 205°F   ⏳5'-7'

When combined with the Hesperides notes of the citrus fruits, the woodland character of Wu Long (oolong) 7 citrus fruits tea takes on a delicious flavour, whilst ret aining its long lasting taste.

REF. 491

THÉ VERT 7 AGRUMES
☀ 🌡 170°F   ⏳3'

'Green tea 7 citrus'. The freshness of the Japanese green tea and the acidulous juicy taste of the citrus fruits are wonderfully balanced. A fresh and vitamin rich blend.

REF. 495

GOÛT RUSSE IMPÉRIAL
☀ 🌡 205°F   ⏳4'-5'

'Imperial Russian blend' is a very fine, classic tea, in which the scent of mandarins and red citrus fruits is predominant.

REF. 492

REMPARTS DE VARSOVIE
☀ 🌡 205°F   ⏳4'-5'

'Warsaw Ramparts'. A fairly lively tea with a predominant flavour of grapefruit.

REF. 489

THÉ AUX ORANGES DE CUBA
☀ 🌡 205°F   ⏳4'-5'

'Cuban orange tea' is a light and delicate tea scented with sweet oranges from Cuba.

REF. 493

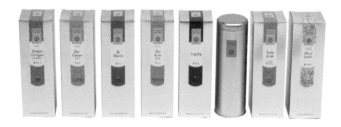

Selection of teas pre-packaged in metal tea canisters. Ref. DVN

▮ FLOWERS
OF CHINA
▮ jasmine teas

Jasmine teas, from the Fujian province, are prepared using green or Wu Long (oolong) teas, to which freshly plucked jasmine flowers are added. The tea leaves easily absorb any scents so they are laid in a container with thin layers of flowers. The receptacle is covered with straw for 24 hours and then heated for an hour before the leaves are separated from the flowers. The fewer flowers, the higher quality of tea.

PERLES DE JASMIN
☀ ♨ 180°F   ⧖ 3'-4'

Very rare and available very sporadically, 'Jasmine Pearls' are produced using best quality green tea leaves. They are rolled by hand into tiny round balls. By being folded in the leaf preserves the delicate fragrance of the jasmine flower with which it was scented. This spectacular tea produces a beverage of the highest quality: the softness of the green tea is the perfect complement to the subtlety of the jasmine. The roundness and the smoothness of the beverage feels like a pearl of tea to the palate.

This ultimate jasmine tea must be taken in its natural state with nothing added, after 3 to 4 minutes brewing.

REF. 248

GRAND JASMIN MAO FENG
☀ ♨ 180°F   ⧖ 3'

'Hair ends'. A very rare jasmine tea, made up mainly of buds. It died out a long time ago but the province of Fujian has started to produce it again in very small quantities. One of the best-made teas as far as jasmine is concerned. There are no flowers: they are all removed so the tea has no bitterness. The mellowness of the liqueur and the subtlety of its scent make it worthy of its status as an exceptional tea.

REF. 249

Blends and flavours

Grand Jasmin Chun Feng
☀ 🌡 170°F   ⏳ 3'

Along with the previous teas, this is one of the best. Here also, almost all the flowers have been removed and there is a high bud count. An outstanding base tea that allows the jasmine scent to be fully released after brewing for three minutes.

REF. 250

IN A TIN (100G): REF. DVN250

IN MUSLIN BAGS: REF. D250S

Grand Jasmin Monkey King
☀ 🌡 180°F   ⏳ 3'

'Harvest of the Monkeys'. Legend has it that monkeys were trained to pick the highest shoots of wild tea plants. Few flowers and a small leaf, like Chun Feng tea.

REF. 251

Fleur de Jasmin
☀ 🌡 180°F   ⏳ 3'

'Jasmine Flower' with white tips and a few flowers.

REF. 252

Jasmin
☀ 🌡 180°F   ⏳ 4'

A good, flowery tea.

REF. 253

▇ rose tea

As with jasmine teas, rose petals are mixed with the tea leaves, except that in this case it is not necessary to remove them, since they do not make the infusion bitter.

Rose de Chine
☀ 🌡 205°F   ⏳ 5'

Qimen tea and rose petals.

LOOSE: REF. 847

AS A DELICE DE THE: REF. F500RO

Spice breads

Our spice breads are home-baked according to a traditional recipe and using the finest ingredients. The method of baking ensures that they remain soft and spongy.
Gingerbread with cherries. REF. F701.
Gingerbread with ginger. REF. F700.

SCENTED BLENDS

mainly floral

THÉ DES MOINES
☀ 🌡 205°F   ⏳3'

Inspired by an ancient recipe handed down by Tibetan monks, Thé des Moines is a floral blend with a unique flavour. Legend tells how the monks would prepare this blend of tea, plants and flowers in the greatest of secrecy.

After several days of soaking, the leaves were carefully plucked out and put to one side. By this mysterious alchemy the monks turned the tea into gold and gave Thé des Moines its exceptional scent.

LOOSE: REF. 898

IN A TIN (100G): REF. DVN898

IN MUSLIN BAGS: REF. D898S

AS A DELICE DE THE: REF. F500MO

IN A TRADITIONAL POT

(SEE P.77): REF. D898P (B, J OR N)

THÉ DES SABLES
☀ 🌡 170°F   ⏳3'

Inspired by a journey to Morocco, Thé des Sables is a blend with a green tea base. The rose of Damascus, a famous rose grown on the slopes of Mount Atlas, is combined with hot weather fruits – mangoes, yellow peaches and citrus fruits – in order to reproduce the unique flavour of a petal jam preserve. Fresh and sensual at the same times it is equally good either piping hot or chilled. (PHOTO P.95)

LOOSE: REF. 858

IN A TIN (100G): REF. DVN858

IN MUSLIN BAGS: REF. D858S

THÉ AUX FLEURS ORIENTALES
☀ 🌡 205°F   ⏳4'-5'

A flowery oriental blend of light Chinese tea, scented with rose and lotus flowers.

REF. 870

IKEBANA
☀ 🌡 205°F   ⏳5'

A flowery blend of green and black teas scented with mint, rose, jasmine and orchid.

REF. 868

THÉ DES SOURCES
☀ 🌡 170°F   ⏳3'-4'

An intense and refreshing blend of China green tea, mint leaves and a touch of bergamot.

LOOSE: REF. 857

IN A TIN (100G): REF. DVN857

IN MUSLIN BAGS: REF. D857S

▩ mainly fruity

THÉ DU HAMMAM
☀ 🌡 170°F   ⏳ 3'

Inspired by a Turkish recipe using green tea, Thé du Hammam is a fruity blend wich evokes the fragrances used to perfume the hammam: roses, green dates, red fruit and orange flower water. Sprinkled with flower petals in the purest of eastern traditions, the tea's extraordinary fragrance features a subtle combination of Chinese green tea, celebrated for its freshness and thirst-quenching properties, and rich fruit aromas.

LOOSE: REF. 861

IN A TIN (100G): REF. DVN861

IN MUSLIN BAGS: REF. D861S

AS A DELICE DE THE: REF. F500HA

THÉ DU HAMMAM "ROOIBOS"
☾ 🌡 205°F   ⏳ 5'

Here, the wonderful flavours of Thé du hammam are combined with the roundness of Rooibos. A fruity and tasty blend, that may be enjoyed at any time of day or evening.

LOOSE: REF. 920

IN A TIN (100G): REF. DVN920

IN MUSLIN BAGS: REF. D920S

THÉ DU HAMMAM BLACK LEAF
☀ 🌡 195°F   ⏳ 5'

A black tea variation of Thé du Hammam wonderful recipe. The rich accents of red fruit and flowers are subtly enlivened by a rhubard note.

LOOSE: REF. 855

IN MUSLIN BAGS: REF. D855S

THÉ DES SONGES
☾ 🌡 205°F   ⏳ 5'-7'

A delicious Wu Long (oolong) that is scented with flowers and exotic fruits.

LOOSE: REF. 896

IN A TIN (100G): REF. DVN896

IN MUSLIN BAGS: REF. D896S

AS A DELICE DE THE: REF: F500MI

Thé des Moines scented candle
Ref. T898

Thé du Hammam scented candle
Ref. T861

Thé des Lords scented candle
Ref. T802

THÉ DES SONGES BLANC

☀ 🌡 180°F   ⏳ 5'-7'

A delicious white tea with safflower petals and strawberry pieces, evoking rose, orange blossom and red fruit. Refined and delicate.

LOOSE: REF. 8965

IN A TIN (100G): REF. DVN8965

THÉ AUX FRUITS D'ÉTÉ

☀ 🌡 205°F   ⏳ 4'-5'

'Summer fruit tea' is a very handsome Yunnan tea, scented with natural extracts of Na-she, a fruit that grows in the south of China with a taste similar to a pear and the shape of a small apple. A fresh and subtle blend, with a scattering of marigold petals.

REF. 873

THÉ DES CONCUBINES

☀ 🌡 205°F   ⏳ 4'-5'

A rare tea, Thé des Concubines is a refined delicate blend of green and black China teas enlivened by rose petals and pieces of fruit, evoking fruity notes of cherry, mango and vanilla. The atmosphere of a Chinese tea house is what we wanted to recapture here.

LOOSE: REF. 864

IN A TIN (100G): REF. DVN864

THÉ DES ALIZÉS

☀ 🌡 170°F   ⏳ 3'

A green tea enlivened by flower petals and delicately scented with pieces of white peach, kiwi and watermelon. The green tea and the juicy freshness of the fruit are wonderfully balanced. Can be drunk hot or iced.

REF. 862

IN A TIN (100G): REF. DVN862

IN MUSLIN BAGS: REF. D862S

THÉ DES ENFANTS

☾ 🌡 205°F   ⏳ 5'

A blend of black tea, pieces of dried fruit and flowers, with a tasty cherry flavour.

REF. 960

IN A TIN (100G): REF. DVN960

THÉOPHILE

☀ 🌡 170°F   ⏳ 3'

Le Palais des Thés celebrates oriental tradition with a deliciously exotic creation. This green tea with fruity accents of lychee and mango, spiced up with a floral note of lotus, can be enjoyed both hot and chilled.

REF. 887

Thé des Concubines scented candle
Ref. T864

Fleur de Geisha scented candle
Ref. T309

Blends and flavours

Forêt Noire
☀ 🌡 205°F   ⏳ 4'-5'

A blend of high altitude teas, enlivened with black fruits, wild berries and blueberry flowers. Blackberry is the dominant note.
REF. 891

Songe d'une nuit d'été
☀ 🌡 205°F

A flowery and fruity black tea, with exotic notes.
REF. 872

Byzance
☀ 🌡 205°F   ⏳ 4'-5'

Blend of black, green, red teas and mate, in which the dominant flavours are blackcurrant and cardamom.
REF. 888

Fruits rouges Wu Long
☾ 🌡 205°F   ⏳ 5'-7'

'Red fruit Wu Long'. Raspberry and wild strawberry.
REF. 884

Tropical Wu Long
☾ 🌡 205°F   ⏳ 5'-7'

A cocktail of tropical fruits and flowers: mango, passion fruit and guava.
REF. 894

Montagne Bleue
☀ 🌡 205°F   ⏳ 4'-5'

Black tea, honey, lavender, blueberry, strawberry and rhubarb.
LOOSE: REF. 889

AS A DELICE DE THE: REF. F500MB

Quatre fruits rouges
☀ 🌡 205°F   ⏳ 4'-5'

'Four red fruit'. Black tea, strawberry, raspberry, cherry and redcurrant.
REF. 885

Thé aux fruits du Népal
☀ 🌡 205°F   ⏳ 4'-5'

'Fruit tea from Népal'. Black tea, lotus, lychee, cinnamon and mango.
REF. 886

▦ mainly citrus

Thé aux fruits d'automne
☀ 🌡 205°F   ⏳ 4'-5'

'Autumn fruit tea'. Black tea, lemon and hibiscus flower.
REF. 878

Gibraltar
☀ 🌡 205°F   ⏳ 4'-5'

Black tea, red citrus fruit, vanilla, honey and spices.
REF. 866

Soirée d'hiver
☀ 🌡 205°F   ⏳ 4'-5'

Black tea, spices, citrus fruit and caramel.
REF. 874

THÉ AUX FRUITS DE LA MÉDITERRANÉE

☀ 🌡 205°F   ⏳ 4'-5'

'Tea with Mediterranean fruit'. Black tea, lavender, mandarin and vanilla.

REF. 882

◼ mainly spicy

N°25

☀ 🌡 205°F   ⏳ 4'-5'

Three superb blends with citrus fruit, rose and spices: vanilla, cinnamon and almond. They are only available over the Christmas/ New Year period.

THÉ N°25 NOIR. LOOSE: REF. 860

IN A TIN (100G): REF. DVN860

THÉ N°25 VERT. LOOSE: REF. 859

THÉ N°25 ROOIBOS. LOOSE: REF. 916

THÉ DES VAHINÉS "ROOIBOS"

☾ 🌡 205°F   ⏳ 5'

A delicious pairing of vanilla and almond, for a warm and sophisticated blend.

LOOSE: REF. 856

IN A TIN (100G): REF. DVN856

IN MUSLIN TEA BAGS: REF. D856S

THÉ DES AMANTS

☀ 🌡 205F   ⏳ 4'-5'

Rich and sensual, a voluptuous and fragrant blend of black tea, apple, almond, cinnamon and vanilla, spiced up with a hint of ginger.

LOOSE: REF. 880

IN A TIN (100G): REF. DVN880

IN MUSLIN TEA BAGS: REF. D880S

THÉ DES AMANTS "ROOIBOS"

☾ 🌡 205°F   ⏳ 5'

Voluptuous, this new version is sure to appeal to fans of Thé des Amants. A very beautiful blend of Rooibos, apple, almond, cinnamon and vanilla, spiced up with a hint of ginger. This tea may be enjoyed at any time of day or evening.

REF. 919

THÉ DES FAKIRS

☀ 🌡 170°F   ⏳ 3'

Inspired by the Chai tradition, Thé des Fakirs is a tasty, scented blend of green tea, cardamom and cloves with a hint of grapefruit.

LOOSE: REF. 875

IN A TIN (100G) : REF. DVN875

IN MUSLIN TEA BAGS: REF. D875S

IN GANESHA CANISTER: REF : D875F

BLENDS AND FLAVOURS

CHAI

☀ 🌡 205°F ⏳4'-5'

A blend of tea and spices, which is infused in boiling milk, with sugar, according to Indian custom.

REF. 770

SAINT-NICOLAS

☀ 🌡 205°F ⏳4'-5'

Black tea, bitter almond, cinnamon and walnuts.

REF. 890

TOFFEE

☀ 🌡 205°F ⏳4'-5'

Black tea with the flavour of the famed English confection, which combines natural essences of vanilla and cocoa.

REF. 865

CACHEMIRE

☀ 🌡 205°F ⏳4'-5'

Blend of black and green teas with citrus fruits and spices: cloves and cinnamon.

REF. 867

Teas and scented blends selection box.
Each tea bag contains around 0,1 oz of tea.
See box-set p.81, 103.

LORELEÏ

☀ 🌡 205°F ⏳4'-5'

Black tea, cinnamon, vanilla and almond.

REF. 871

MEKONG

☀ 🌡 205°F ⏳4'-5'

A black tea scented with fruits that grow along river banks: the Indochinese pear, ginger, citrus fruits and mint.

REF. 869

■ **mainly iodised**

THÉ MARIN

☾ 🌡 205°F ⏳5'-7'

'Marine Tea' is an astonishing blend of semi fermented teas and algae. High in mineral salts and trace elements essential to the proper functioning of the body (iron, iodine, calcium, magnesium and phosphor), its benefits are prized by oriental dietary specialists. Low in theine, it should be allowed to brew for 5 to 7 minutes and may be enjoyed at any time of day or evening.

REF. 899

FLAVOURED TEAS

APRICOT
REF. 740   🌡 205°F ☀ ⏳ 4'-5'

BERGAMOT *(see Earl Grey p. 104)*

CARAMEL
REF. 750   🌡 205°F ☀ ⏳ 4'-5'

CARDAMOM
REF. 751   🌡 205°F ☀ ⏳ 4'-5'

CINNAMON
REF. 749   🌡 205°F ☀ ⏳ 4'-5'

COCONUT
REF. 822   🌡 205°F ☀ ⏳ 4'-5'

GINGER
REF. 781   🌡 205°F ☀ ⏳ 4'-5'

GINSENG
REF. 782   🌡 205°F ☀ ⏳ 4'-5'

JASMINE *(see Flowers of China p.112)*

LIME SENCHA
REF. 766   🌡 170°F ☀ ⏳ 3'

LIME WU LONG
REF. 765   🌡 205°F ☾ ⏳ 5'-7'

LOTUS
REF. 790   🌡 205°F ☀ ⏳ 4'-5'

LYCHEE
REF. 792   🌡 205°F ☀ ⏳ 4'-5'

MANGO
REF. 810   🌡 205°F ☀ ⏳ 4'-5'

MINTED GREEN TEA
   🌡 170°F ☀ ⏳ 4'-5'

LOOSE: REF. 815

IN MUSLIN BAGS: REF. D815S

ORANGE BLOSSOM WU LONG
REF. 824   🌡 205°F ☾ ⏳ 5'-7'

PASSION FRUIT
REF. 779   🌡 205°F ☀ ⏳ 4'-5'

PEACH
REF. 833   🌡 205°F ☀ ⏳ 4'-5'

ROSE *(see Flowers of China p.112)*

GREEN TEA WITH VANILLA
LOOSE REF. 850   🌡 170°F ☀ ⏳ 3'

IN MUSLIN TEA BAGS REF. D850S

VANILLA
REF. 849   🌡 205°F ☀ ⏳ 4'-5'

VIOLET
REF. 851   🌡 205°F ☀ ⏳ 4'-5'

WILD STRAWBERRY
REF. 776   🌡 205°F ☀ ⏳ 4'-5'

DECAFFEINATED TEAS

NATURAL
REF. 901   🌡 205°F ☾ ⏳ 4'-5'

PRACTICAL ADVICE

■ HOW SHOULD TEA BE PREPARED?

To use tea properly, it is important to understand its particular characteristics. Indeed there are as many ways of preparing tea as there are different varieties. The criteria governing the amount of tea used, the length of infusion and the temperature and even the quality of the water will vary depending on the tea's origin, the season, the fineness of the crop or local custom. For this reason every time you buy tea from Le Palais des Thés we will provide you with the appropriate and precise advice necessary for preparing it correctly. Furthermore, owing to their many properties, teas can be more suitable for certain times of the day. This is why Le Palais des Thés has deemed it useful to give you this information about each one of our teas by using the symbols that you will find next to each description.

The infusion chart opposite gives you a broad outline for preparing tea, according to its colour and its origin. Please refer to the individual descriptions of each tea for more precise instructions, in order to find out if there are any local customs or special ways of drinking it.

■ THE CHOICE OF WATER

The choice of water is often something that is not considered in the preparation of tea. However using a good quality water is essential in order to fully appreciate the fineness and the subtlety of a tea.

Tap water is often mediocre from a taste point of view, owing to the products that have been added to it to make it safe for drinking, especially chlorine. A filtration system that decreases the hardness of the water can be used to resolve this problem.

INFUSION CHART	Infusion Temperature	Infusion Time	Quantity per 5 fl oz
White Teas			
• Aiguilles d'argent	160°F	5 to 10 mn	0.2 oz
• Bai Mu Dan	180°F	5 to 10 mn	0.2 oz
Green Teas			
• New season Chinese green teas	160°F-170°F	2 to 4 mn	0.2 oz
• Other Chinese green teas	160°F-170°F	3 to 5 mn	0.1 oz
• Japanese green teas	105°F-180°F *according to the quality*	1 to 3 mn	0.2 oz
Wu Long (oolong) teas			
• Gong Fu Cha method	205°F	*For between 20 seconds and 1 minute per infusion*	*Fill the teapot a third full with tea leaves*
• in a traditional teapot	205°F	5 to 7 mn	0.2 oz
Black teas			
• China	180°F-205°F	3 to 5 mn	0.2 oz
• India, *Darjeeling first flush*	180°F-185°F	2 to 4 mn	0.3 to 0.4 oz
• India, *Darjeeling other flushes*	180°F-205°F	3 to 5 mn	0.3 to 0.4 oz
• India, Assam	180°F-205°F	3 to 5 mn	0.2 oz
• Sri Lanka and other sources	180°F-205°F	3 to 5 mn	0.2 oz
Dark teas	205°F	4 to 5 mn	0.2 oz
Scented teas			
• black tea base	180°F-205°F	4 to 5 mn	0.2 oz
• semi-fermented tea base	205°F	5 to 7 mn	0.2 oz
• green tea base	170°F	3 to 4 mn	0.2 oz
• smoked teas	180°F-205°F	3 to 4 mn	0.2 oz
• jasmine teas	160°F-170°F	3 to 4 mn	0.2 oz
Rooibos	205°F	5 mn	0.2 oz

For the best tea it is recommended that mineral water or spring water be used. Spring water containing few minerals will act as a neutral base, which will bring out the strong taste qualities of the tea. Mineral water will bring its own flavour to the tea, something that may not necessarily be detrimental to its taste. For example, slightly acidic waters work very well with spring Darjeelings.

The temperature of the water is another aspect that is all too frequently neglected. The water should never be poured over the tea leaves at boiling point: this would burn them and destroy the aroma molecules that they contain, thus robbing the tea of the very essence of its bouquet. For certain very fragile teas it is even important not to overheat the water so as to preserve the delicacy of the leaf.

HOW CAN I DECAFFEINATE MY TEA?

There is nothing simpler than decaffeinating one's own tea! It is possible to do so with all teas, without exception:

• pour some water, at the correct temperature, over the leaves and allow to infuse for 30 seconds,
• after 30 seconds pour this water away,
• pour some fresh water over the same leaves and allow to infuse as usual.

Caffeine is released during the very first seconds of infusion. So by throwing away the first water the caffeine has therefore gone. Nevertheless it would be a pity to decaffeinate a rare tea since this would mean losing some of its character.

ICED TEA

Infuse 0,3 to 0,4 oz of tea in a litre of water at room temperature overnight. The tea obtained in this way will be full-bodied with a very pronounced flavour. Then refrigerate. This method of preparation is ideally suited to the great black teas. Before serving add a twist of orange or a little piece of lime to enhance the flavour.

For scented teas and blends it is recommended that 0,5 to 0,7 oz of tea are infused in one litre of cold water, for one hour in the case of black tea-based blends (Goût Russe 7 agrumes, Thé des Concubines) and half an hour for green tea-based blends (Thé du Hammam, Thé des Alizés, Thé des Sables). Then keep refrigerated.

HOW TO BECOME A THÉOPHILE?

Théophiles are privilege members of Le Palais des Thés. By becoming a Théophile you will become eligible for many special offers both in our stores and on the Internet or by mail.

You will also benefit from special privileges at L'école du Thé. Finally you will be regularly kept up to date about a subject that is close to your heart — tea — by our newsletter.

pass a mail order or order on the Internet Le Palais des Thés will make sure this is done for you. You become a Théophile if you spend 80 euros or more on loose tea during the course of one year.

YOUR THÉOPHILE CARD

YOUR LOYALTY CARD

Remember to have your loyalty card stamped each time you visit one of our stores. Each time you

Your Théophile card will entitle you to a 10% discount on all our products (except on books: official discount of 5%) for one whole year at all Le Palais des Thés stores as well as on the Internet or by mail. You will also receive our newsletter Bruits de Palais™, which enables you to be the first to discover new teas, stay up to date on the latest news about this beverage (medical research, cultivation...) and take advantage of many special offers. Your Théophile card will also allow you to enjoy preferential rates and priority admission to L'école du Thé lectures.

Recognised for its expertise in the field of tea, Le Palais des Thés created in 1999 L'École du Thé out of a desire to share its know-how, its passion and its experiences of tea.

Given the complexity of their profession, expert tea tasters fascinate us with their individual talent and wealth of experience.

Nevertheless, appreciating the subtlety of a green tea from China, comparing two Darjeelings plucked within days of one another and evaluating the climatic conditions under which a given tea has been grown are not inaccessible goals.

In our cultures, our sense of smell and taste are required relatively rarely and are therefore barely developed. However, when we start to learn more about tea, training ourselves to smell and taste, our senses are capable of making rapid and spectacular progress…procuring unrivalled tea-drinking pleasure!

With L'École du Thé, Le Palais des Thés offers an initiation into the art of tasting. Guided by our experts, you too can become a veritable connoisseur, capable of appreciating the slightest nuance of a grand cru and recognising the simplicity of mass-produced teas.

L'École du Thé programme consists of two approaches:
• *ten tasting initiation modules*, taking you on a chronological journey, best followed from start to finish,
• *a series of varying levels of training sessions* which are developed in accordance with the seasons, new arrivals and your personal preferences.

Since tea also opens doors to the people and cultures of the world, L'École du Thé will allow you to meet other tea enthusiasts and participate in tea ceremonies, as well as discovering the art and civilisations linked to this wonderful beverage. You will even have access to recipes and advice from top chefs who use tea in their cuisine.

L'École du thé - The tea school

Discover the 10 modules which consist of learning tea-testing and finding more about the most important tea producing countries:

Module I
what is tea?
Follow the path taken by tea leaves from the tea bush to your cup, and learn to distinguish various tea-production methods.

Module II to V
Learn about the key factors that contribute to the success of tea-tasting, gain a better understanding for the role played by each of our senses in this process.
• The ideal conditions for tea-tasting
• Understanding tasting
• Expressing yourself
• Tasting techniques

Module VI to X
Discover the specific features of teas from each major country of origin. The themes covered include history, the properties of individual teas, economic and social issues.
• Chinese teas
• Japanese teas
• Taiwanese teas
• Indian teas
• Blends and Flavoured Teas

Children's Module
(6-12 years old)
View L'École du Thé programme online: www.palaisdesthes.com

L'Ecole du Thé
7 rue de Nice, 75011 Paris
Tel: +33 (0)1 43 56 90 90
Fax: +33 (0)1 43 56 92 00
E-mail: ecole@palaisdesthes.com

DISCOVERING TEA with François-Xavier Delmas
A Tea Traveller's Blog

A tireless traveller, François-Xavier Delmas has journeyed the world for more than 20 years in search of the finest teas. Through India, China, Nepal, Japan, Taiwan and Sri lanka, he has scaled mountains and crossed valleys on his quest for the rarest leaves. He created his blog to share his passion. www.discoveringtea.com invites you to follow his daily peregrinations. It is also an opportunity to experience, almost «live», the tasting sessions of the spring teas in the plantations, his meetings with small producers, and so on. A keen photographer, François-Xavier travels the tea routes for more than half the year, and captures the important moments of the tea harvests on camera. His blog is full of beautiful photos that show how, beyond the quest for tea itself, his journey is all about discovering other people, other traditions: the cultures of the world. François-Xavier will introduce you to the people he works with, many of whom are longstanding friends. His blog is vibrant, rich and captivating, like tea itself. It is also an opportunity to share thoughts with others, to communicate directly with François-Xavier, to ask him questions about his travels, and about tea. So please feel free to give your opinion, or leave a comment!

How can i buy tea?

Le Palais des Thés shops

In Le Palais des Thés shops you will find all the teas described in this guide, as well as a large selection of artefacts, accessories and delicacies from many different countries where serving tea is a time-honoured tradition. Our enthusiastic, specialized sales staff will welcome you with a cup of tea and are always on hand to answer any questions you might have, offer advice on which teas to try and generally pass on a little of the expertise we have gleaned from our travels around the world's tea plantations.

The layout of the shops allows customers to wander freely and discover the various teas in their own time, with many samples available to smell and taste as well as all kinds of information on their origins, preparation and ceremonies.

▪ WWW. PALAISDESTHES.COM

www.palaisdesthes.com, our website is both an on-line shop and an educational site that provides an alternative way to find out about tea.

All our teas have been photographed and are accompanied by advice on the best way to drink them: in other words you can explore them just as you would if you were in one of our shops - and we do our utmost to make you forget that you can't smell their bouquet!

Specialized software allows you to select teas according to your own requirements such as the origin of the tea, the time of day you wish to drink it, the vitamin and caffeine content and so on. Whatever your need, a selection of teas will be offered, making your choice much easier. Ordering is very straightforward via a secure payment system. Théophile card holders will enjoy the usual discounts by quoting their membership number.

If you sign up to the website's mailing list, you will receive regular updates by e-mail on all aspects of tea: Le Palais des Thés news, recipes using tea, the health benefits of tea, etc.

▪ MAIL ORDER
+33 (0)1 43 56 90 90

This guide has been developed to help you choose your teas. If you need guidance, please contact our sales team at any time by mail. They will give you further information on anything to do with the teas, artefacts and accessories we sell and will fully answer any questions you might have.

On page 128, you will find all the practical help you need to place your order.

INDEX